D0063586

THE SAVVY
SCREENWRITER

HOW TO
SELL YOUR
SCREENPLAY
(AND YOURSELF)
WITHOUT
SELLING OUT!

SUSAN KOUGUELL

"If you make your living as a screenwriter (or simply hope to!) you need this book. Susan Kouguell has helped countless writers take their craft to the next level. I know because I'm one of them!"
— Dan Brown
National best-selling author of
"Digital Fortress" and "Angels and Demons"

"An invaluable resource for screenwriters. Thorough, practical and easy to follow, *The Savvy Screenwriter* should be on the bookshelf of every aspiring screenwriter."
— Nina Streich
Former Deputy Film Commissioner, City of New York

"Full of savvy advice about the screenwriting trade, Kouguell's humorous anecdotes from the front line are themselves well worth the price of admission. Strong on the fundamentals of craft, as well as business protocol, the book left me wishing it had been available when I was just starting out in the biz."
— Will Scheffer
Playwright/screenwriter "Easter," and "In the Gloaming"

"Kouguell is simply one of the most original and exciting writers I know. Her insights into the craft, and business of screenwriting in *The Savvy Screenwriter* are pure gold."
— Carl Capotorto
Playwright/screenwriter, Chesterfield winner,
3-time O'Neill playwriting fellow

"The quintessential how-to book for anyone starting off in the business of writing screenplays. Kouguell has taken all the unspoken rules of our beguiling business and summarized them in a breezy, fun-to-read primer. Before you write one word of your screenplay, read *The Savvy Screenwriter*. It will save you countless missteps."
— Doug Witkins
President, Picture This! Entertainment,
and Highland Crest Pictures

THE SAVVY SCREENWRITER

How to Sell Your Screenplay (and Yourself) Without Selling Out!

Susan Kouguell

For information, contact TL Hoell Books, 1 Colonial Way,
Exeter, NH 03833. Or visit us on the World Wide Web at
www.tlhoellbooks.com

Updated information about selling your script, Susan
Kouguell's seminars, and contacting the author, can be found at
www.savvyscreenwriter.com

Interested in learning more about Su-City Pictures East and
private consultations? Contact Susan Kouguell at
info@su-city-pictures.com
or visit us on the World Wide Web at
www.su-city-pictures.com

Book and cover design by Craig Lowy Design.

Library of Congress Cataloging-in-Publication Data

Kouguell, Susan.

The Savvy Screenwriter: How to Sell Your Screenplay (and
Yourself) Without Selling Out! /Susan Kouguell

ISBN 0-9679948-0-2
Library of Congress Catalog Card Number 00-131903.

Printed in the United States of America.

First Edition 2000

FOR

JIM AND TATIANA

ACKNOWLEDGEMENTS

Way back in 1999, something strange happened.

Almost simultaneously, several of my clients, my students from Harvard and at the seminars I presented, wanted to take me home with them. They wanted round-the-clock advice and information about screenwriting, but more than that – they wanted reassurance that they could survive the business of trying to sell their work. Since I had my own family to go home to, I wrote this book instead. *The Savvy Screenwriter* is for them and for anyone else who's been there.

Without my students and clients, and their endless (and often surprising) questions, I don't think I would have written this book. And without the help of my many friends, family, and colleagues, I certainly would have never finished it. It was heartwarming that so many people helped me out as this book took shape. I thank them all – students, clients, colleagues, friends, and family. Amongst all those who helped, the following deserve special praise.

Craig Lowy* for his inspiring feedback, incredible patience, and the dazzling layout and design of this book. Amy Chartoff,* Margie Wachtel, and Judi Rothberg* for their great copyediting. Nancy Carey for her solid proofreading. Dan Brown* and Donnaldson Brown* for their terrific feedback and assistance. Bonnie Bluh, Blythe Brown, Jim Hoell,* Robert C. Levine, Esq.,* and Rose Ann Miller* at Harvard University Press for their generous support and invaluable advice.

My thanks to the Writers Guild of America for inviting me to speak at their Screenwriting Conference in 1993. Special thanks to Bill Lattanzi, who brought along his close friend, Jim, to the event. Jim and I first met at the conference and we married two years later. (The added perk for an already great gig!)

My heartfelt thanks to Jim, who, on a daily basis, cheers me on and encourages me to follow my dreams. To my parents for "enabling" my addiction to movies and their unwavering support. To my grandmother, Omi, who treated us to Thai food regularly when I was too tired to cook, takes full credit for any and all of my successes, and can't understand why Jim puts up with me. And finally, to our four-year-old daughter, Tatiana (perhaps a future screenwriter, but already quite the actress), whose great sense of humor and vivid imagination is a constant inspiration.

* Indicates screenwriter!

TABLE OF CONTENTS

APPENDICES

PREFACE
Empower Yourself

Bravo! You've completed your screenplay. Now what?

Forewarned is forearmed. You need to be ready for what lies ahead.

The Savvy Screenwriter reveals what's in store for you. It demystifies the film business and tells you what you really want and need to know... how to sell your screenplay and yourself without selling out.

Whether your goal is to write for independent or Hollywood films, *The Savvy Screenwriter* will help you to gain an understanding of how the industry works and what it expects from you and your screenplay. A savvy screenwriter is empowered. You must know what you're in for and what you must do if you are going to succeed in the film industry.

When I was brainstorming with my family and friends for a title for this book, one idea I came up with (but which was quickly shot down due to its incredible length) was:

"Everything you always wanted to know about selling your script, finding and working with agents and entertainment attorneys, writing queries and synopses, pitching, learning the psychology of story analysts and movie executives, understanding option agreements and development deals, tackling writing assignments and collaborations, learning the film lingo and resources ... but didn't know whom to ask."

Okay, it was a really long title, but this is what I wanted this book to give you. And here I get the last word – or words.

In my years working on independent and Hollywood films, I endured a number of bumps and bruises, but through trial and error I finally figured out how things worked. *The Savvy Screenwriter* will help you navigate the maze set up by the film industry, which is filled with daunting rules, etiquette, and the secret society of film executives. If only I'd had a book like this, a book that would have empowered and guided me through this often difficult maze, I would have been able to devote more time to writing and less to tending to my bumps and bruises. And I would have had a lot more fun learning the film industry ropes.

If I had known then what I know now...

Throughout *The Savvy Screenwriter* you'll find personal anecdotes from my past. (They are typed like this, on my old-fashioned typewriter.) The movie scenes (typed in screenplay format) are *fictionalized* accounts of often sad but true events that happened to me in the film business – many of which occurred when I first started out. People's names and titles of films have often been omitted to protect my pocketbook and my career.

INTRODUCTION

You've probably heard that "everyone has a screenplay in his or her drawer," and this doesn't seem to be an exaggeration. Since 1990 when I started my consulting company, which later became Su-City Pictures East, I've worked with over 1,000 clients including Emmy-winning and Oscar-nominated writers and filmmakers, as well as surgeons, CEOs, journalists, food critics, sales clerks, dentists, lawyers, optometrists, artists, musicians, police officers, and even a well-known dominatrix. But despite varied backgrounds, they've all had one thing in common – they wanted to get their scripts produced.

THE CLIENT COUCH

```
I have a couch at my Su-City Pictures East
office. On occasion, clients have become so
comfortable with me that they'll collapse on
my couch, spill out their guts, and reveal
their deep dark secrets, asking for advice
not only about their scripts but also on
how to survive the difficult life of a
writer.  They treat me like a therapist,
and I know from my own emotionally draining
battles with the film industry that they
probably need one.
```

Sometimes it all seems to be an exasperating test – a test of your self-esteem, your ability to accept rejection, to take criticism and you'll need a strong stomach to ride the roller coaster of near misses. If you are ready for the ride of your life – and maybe want to avoid a real licensed-therapist's couch – then *The Savvy Screenwriter* is for you.

Understanding how the film industry works and how to navigate it may seem like an impossible task, but if you follow my step-by-step advice, you will discover the road best traveled. Or, you can use this book as a map – jumping to topics you are particularly interested in, since each chapter in *The Savvy Screenwriter* is self-contained. (This means that some information is repeated.)

FACTS AND FAQ'S ABOUT THE BUSINESS OF SCREEN-WRITING

You have questions – and lots of them! In Chapter 1, I'll answer the most commonly asked questions about the business of screenwriting. With your basic questions answered, you'll be ready to meet the industry professionals who are going to read your script.

HOW TO MAKE A STORY ANALYST LOVE YOU AND YOUR SCRIPT

Chapter 2 reveals story analysts' secrets. It shows you who they are, what they are looking for, and how to deliver a script that they will love. In Chapter 3, the story analysts' coverage (story report) is explained. Here you will discover how a story analyst reads your script and learn what is included in the story report.

FINE-TUNING YOUR SCRIPT

How can you tell if your script is *really* finished and ready to be sent out? Chapter 4 offers all the essential tools and checklists for preparing your final polish.

GETTING YOUR CAREER IN GEAR

Now that your script is perfect, it's time to get down to business – the film business. In Chapters 5, 6, and 7, you will find the elusive key to unlocking the mysterious film business door; learn all the do's and don'ts about writing a great query and a sensational synopsis; then discover how to prepare yourself and your pitch for that all-important meeting with film executives.

MARKETING YOURSELF AND YOUR SCRIPT

You may have a fabulous script, but it's not going to do any good if it's sitting in your desk drawer. Chapter 8 includes advice on developing a "Hit List" of companies and agents. It gives you savvy shortcuts to networking, and additional suggestions for screenplay opportunities. While you're doing all this groundwork, you need to seek representation. Chapter 9 shows you how to find an agent and, once you get one, how best to work together to sell your script and get writing assignments. If you are waiting for an agent's response or can't find an agent, there are other options. An entertainment attorney can submit your script and look out for your best interests; all of this is covered in Chapter 10.

GETTING ASSIGNMENTS AND SURVIVING WITH DIGNITY

When you finally receive the attention you deserve for your screenplay, it's imperative to understand the opportunities and traps that lie ahead. Chapter 11 covers the basics of the Option Agreement and the Development Deal in language that you will understand. Since filmmaking is a collaborative process, you must know how to work with producers, directors, and actors. Chapter 12 gives you hands-on advice to help you succeed in your writing assignments and collaborations. Chapter 13 provides essential pointers for the savvy screenwriter from insights into contracts to making the most of your screenwriting career. And finally, Chapter 14 offers some advice about the adventure you are about to embark on.

SCREENWRITING RESOURCES AND LINGO

The savvy screenwriter is well-versed in all aspects of the film industry. To keep you in the know, Appendix A defines vital terminology and Appendix B lists resources and organizations.

THE SAVVY SCREENWRITER

How to Sell Your Screenplay
(and Yourself)
Without Selling Out!

Susan Kouguell

CHAPTER ONE

YOUR QUESTIONS – MY ANSWERS

Here are the questions most commonly posed by my clients, students, and seminar attendees about working in and surviving the film business.

What exactly is a spec script?
A spec script is a screenplay that is written on speculation – meaning without payment or before a deal has been negotiated.

How likely is it that I will sell my spec script?
To be honest, selling a script is like winning the lottery. Someone has to win the lottery... and some writers do sell their scripts! To keep sane and focused against such staggering odds, it's important to keep in mind three potential

goals. You want: 1) to get your script sold; 2) to get your script produced; and 3) to have it serve as a writing sample for future work.

What are the steps to getting my spec script sold?

1. Write a great script. *(See Chapter 4.)*
2. Write a strong query letter that will entice an executive to want to read your script. *(See Chapter 5.)*
3. Compose a strong synopsis that demonstrates why your story is great. *(See Chapter 6.)*
4. Write a powerful pitch that will inspire an executive to buy your idea and/or script. *(See Chapter 7.)*
5. Target the production companies, studios, and talent (actors, directors, producers) that are appropriate for your script. *(See Appendix B for listings of directories.)*
6. You've heard the joke: "What's the best way to Carnegie Hall? ... Practice. Practice. Practice." What's the best way to break into the film business? "Network. Network. Network." Writing is solitary, but the film industry is all about connections. No matter where you live, you must find a way to make personal contacts with industry professionals. *(See Chapter 8.)*
7. Find representation. Learn how to find agents and entertainment attorneys, and discover how they can work for and with you. *(See Chapters 9 and 10.)*

A Client's Calling

One of my clients recently told me, "I've been calling everyone that has any remote connection to the film industry, and I'm getting to the point where I'm calling anyone who's ever seen a movie!"

His determination has been paying
off. His script is now in the hands of a
top executive at a major studio.

What exactly is the Writers Guild of America (WGA), and who can join?
The WGA is a labor union that represents approximately 11,000 writers. Eligibility is open to those who have sold literary material to, or are employed by, a signatory – a company that has signed the Guild's Minimum Basic Agreement (MBA). The MBA determines how you work, your writing fee, and additional fees when your work is reused on basic cable, free TV, videocassettes, and interactive media.

Members living east of the Mississippi belong to WGA East and members living west of the Mississippi belong to WGA West. Every member works under the same contracts and receives the same benefits.

What type of services does the WGA provide to non-members?
The following is a brief overview of what the WGA provides. Contact or look at their Web site *(see Appendix B)* for additional services:

- **Registration.** It's imperative to register your script, treatment, and/or synopsis *before* submitting it to any agent, production company, or studio in order to prevent accidental theft of material. You may register your work for a period of five years, after which time you may renew for an additional five years at the current registration fee. If you live east of the Mississippi, register your work with the WGA East, and if you live west of the Mississippi, register your work with the WGA West. *(See Appendix B for addresses.)*

- **Agency List**. The Guild Signatory Agents and Agencies List can be purchased through the WGA at a nominal cost.

How many rewrites do I need to do before I finish my spec script?
I hear this question on a daily basis, and it's usually prefaced with, "I know you don't know the answer but..."

There is no definitive answer. It depends on your own gut instincts, along with the feedback you are getting from a script consultant and/or film executive. You may be able to nail your script in a couple of drafts or it may take thirty drafts or more. The number of rewrites is not a reflection of how talented you are.

How much money can a beginning screenwriter expect to make by selling a spec script?
It depends on the market, the type of picture it is, and who's buying: a Hollywood studio, which could offer thousands of dollars or more, or an independent production company, which could pay you significantly less. Generally, first time screenwriters are offered Writers Guild minimum for a project, which is approximately $30,000 for a low-budget film ($2.5 million and under) or approximately $60,000 for a high-budget film (over $2.5 million). The days of selling a spec script for $1 million-plus seem to be numbered!

Are Hollywood studios open to receiving scripts from writers who don't have agents or previous screenwriting credits?
It's very unlikely that any studio will read a script not submitted by an agent (otherwise known as an unsolicited script), especially if the writer hasn't had a script produced before. Studios are deluged with scripts on an hourly basis, and they rely on agents as a screening mechanism.

Do I have any options if I don't have an agent or can't afford an entertainment attorney to submit my script to a studio or production company?

If you have a connection to an industry professional, sometimes a personal recommendation may help to break down the barrier. *(See Chapter 8.)*

What are managers, and do they do the same job as agents?

Like agents, managers work with writers to strategize their careers and set up pitch meetings with interested companies and talent. Here is where their jobs differ:

- Managers' commissions are usually 15% of what their clients earn, whereas WGA signatory agents can only charge 10%.
- Managers do not negotiate deals on behalf of their clients, whereas agents do negotiate deals.
- Managers can produce scripts written by their clients, but agents who are signatory to the WGA cannot. *(See Chapter 9 for more details about agents.)*

What happens after I send my query letter?

While you are anxiously waiting by the telephone and your mailbox for a reply:

1. An executive's assistant reads your query.
2. If he or she thinks that the company will be interested in your script, it will be passed on to the executive.
3. If the executive is interested, you or your agent (if you have one) will be contacted to submit your synopsis and/or spec script.
4. If the executive likes your synopsis and/or spec script, you or your agent will be contacted to set up a meeting, at which time you may be asked to pitch additional projects.

What exactly is a release form and should I be afraid to sign on the dotted line?
A release form is a legal document that protects production companies and studios from charges of theft of ideas. If a company/studio reads your query letter and is interested in reading your script, generally it will send you a release form to sign. Chances are they will not read your script unless you sign the release.

If the release form is from an established and reputable production company or studio, you should not be afraid to sign on the dotted line. However, if you have *any* doubts or questions, contact an entertainment attorney to review the release form with you.

If I am interested in directing my script, is it worthwhile to make a short film to get attention for my work?
Absolutely. Writing, producing and/or directing a short film can be a useful calling card.

How do you survive having your script almost get produced...?
Have a strong tolerance level for disappointment and lots of stamina! Being in the film industry means developing a high threshold for pain.

AGONIZING CLOSE CALLS

```
I have had countless close calls where
producers and/or directors optioned my work
and I almost had my original scripts
produced... but didn't. There are so many
variables that are out of one's control.
These examples could almost be considered
funny if they weren't so tragic: Private
financing fell through days before shooting
```

```
began, a producer for another script died
during pre-production and the production
shut down, a lead actor dropped out at the
eleventh hour when he received a better
offer and the producers couldn't move
forward without that particular talent
because of a pre-sale distribution agreement
based on the star's participation. And the
list goes on. But sometimes it all comes
together and it's okay. Films that I had
lost hope for actually did get made.
```

What exactly is a treatment?

A treatment is a detailed overview of a screenplay or script idea, which is used as a marketing tool for both spec and for-hire screenwriters to sell their project.

Your treatment should:

- excite the reader to want to read your screenplay;
- be a clear and accurate reflection of your screenplay;
- be written in prose;
- be anywhere from two to fifty pages or more;
- be written in the present tense and paragraph form;
- clearly convey your three acts, but do not label them as such;
- follow your main character's journey;
- include the major plot points;
- illustrate action and description;
- include snippets of dialogue using quotation marks.

Your treatment should not:

- use screenplay format;
- include minor characters or subplots unless requested by film executive;
- include author's editorial comments;
- include characters' inner thoughts.

Do I need to write a treatment?
It's not really necessary to write a treatment along with your spec script unless it assists you in the writing process. Studios and/or production companies usually request treatments *after* you pitch a project idea to them. They will then tell you how many pages to make your treatment. (An average treatment length is thirty pages.) Your treatment should be registered with the WGA prior to submitting it to companies for consideration.

Is a treatment the same as a synopsis?
Although a treatment and a synopsis are both marketing tools to sell your script or script idea, they are not the same. A treatment is a more comprehensive and detailed overview, while a synopsis is generally one page and includes only the very broad strokes of your script. *(See Chapter 6.)*

If I have ideas for music, should I include them in my script?
You may make *suggestions* if – and only if – it's absolutely necessary to your story, but be sure to identify them as just that. Potential producers and directors don't want to be told what music should be in their movie. Additionally, securing music rights can be difficult and very expensive.

If I put a graphic design on the front cover of my script, will this spark executives' attention?
Generally, industry executives do not feel that this enhances

the chances of bringing attention to your script. Executives are interested in your screenplay, not the cover art.

I have an idea for a sequel to a blockbuster film, but is it worth the risk to write it?
Unless you are looking to use this *only* as a writing sample, it is not worth the risk. Chances are the producers of the block-buster film already have a sequel in development. More important, it's highly unlikely that you would be able to obtain the rights to the material, so it's not really worth your time.

How do you handle working with temperamental and difficult well-known talent?
Don't be a doormat! Don't let yourself be intimidated because you're working with a "famous" star. Always stand up for yourself so you're not stepped on.

THE PRIMA DONNA

I've worked with many name actors, producers, and directors either as a screenwriter, Su-City Pictures East consultant, or as an associate producer. Generally, most were great, but there were times on projects where the talent was very challenging to work with. As in any business, it all depends on the individual's personality.

When I worked in the casting department at Paramount Pictures, a famous teen actress was decimating a long line of hapless young male actors for the role of her love interest. After each interval of five auditions, the actress would emerge

```
from the audition room and demand a soft
drink or snack, addressing me as if I were
hearing impaired and a dimwit. She would
then complain to her mother about her
exhaustion and boredom. After each outburst,
her mother plied the young prima donna with
presents - a necklace, earrings, etc. - and
then gently coaxed her daughter back into
the audition room.
        In one way I was lucky. Her mother
went home with her every day and I didn't
have to. Eventually, others tired of her
behavior. The young star's career took a
nosedive. And I'm still here to tell the tale.
```

How do you feel about independent producers and production companies seeking writers through the Internet?

In many ways this is a very positive new venue as writers and producers have a greater access to talent. As with any prospective production company or producer, one must be careful and research who these companies are *prior* to submitting any material.

- Find out how long they have been in business, and if they are financed or have financing.
- Contact them to get references.
- Use common sense. Trust your instincts. If they are evasive, they probably have something to hide.
- Always register your script with the WGA and copyright it *before* submission. *(See Appendix B.)*

Is the Internet a good resource for researching agents and companies?

There is a wealth of useful information on the Internet about new companies, agents, screenplay competitions, script conferences, film festivals, and writing opportunities. *(See Appendix B.)*

Do I have to live in Los Angeles to find work as a screenwriter?
Living in Los Angeles offers more opportunities since that's the town where most deals and movies are made. However, it depends on what type of work you are seeking. For more commercial projects, living in Los Angeles is certainly advantageous, but if your work is more "art-house," an L.A. address isn't a must. Given today's technology, you can really work anywhere if you are willing to hop on a plane to have meetings.

To Live and Work in Los Angeles

After returning from an extended trip to Los Angeles to complete a post-production consulting job for a client, I met with Louis Malle for coffee to catch up. I told him that for the first time I was feeling somewhat torn about living in Manhattan, because it seemed that every time I went to Los Angeles I would be immediately offered very well-paid work. I confided that I really didn't like being in L.A. and would always be a born-and-bred New Yorker. Louis looked me right in the eyes and said, "I know you, Susan, and your writing. If you move to Los Angeles they will eat you up. You will never write again." I heeded his advice and remained living in New York working on the projects I wanted to work on, and traveling to Los Angeles for meetings and assignments. For me, and the

```
type of projects I wanted to work on, this
was the best option.
```

How do I find a script consultant?
The best way to find a good consultant is through word of
mouth. Ask for references. Script consultants advertise in film
magazines, and teach and/or speak at screenwriting conferences. The author of this book works as a script consultant; to
learn more about Su-City Pictures East's script consulting services and to read clients' testimonials contact:
www.su-city-pictures.com

What should I expect from a script consultant's services?
- **Hands-on tools:** A consultant should suggest solutions
  to problems with story, characters, dialogue, structure,
  and genre.
- **Objectivity:** A good consultant will give objective feedback, letting you know what the industry expects of your
  script and to what degree your script meets these expectations.
- **A comfort zone:** It's imperative that you feel comfortable with a consultant and not intimidated by him or
  her. The consultant should provide a safe and non-
  threatening environment, yet be honest with you,
  telling you not just what you want to hear, but what you
  need to hear.
- **Industry knowledge:** A good consultant should have
  extensive experience in the film industry. Your goal is to
  have your script ready for submission, so your consultant should be able to advise you whether it's
  appropriate to take the independent or Hollywood route
  and what to expect from both.

I keep reading and hearing stories about producers, directors, and studios rewriting and often ruining screenwriters' original scripts. If this is true, why do I need to put so much effort into making my script perfect?

Yes, it's true, scripts often do get rewritten by others and the results are sometimes disastrous and often far away from the screenwriters' original intention. But don't use this as an excuse not to make your script the best it can be. Your script is your calling card. It's a reflection of your writing talent.

EATING MY WORDS

```
INT. POSH MANHATTAN RESTAURANT - NIGHT

Crowded and dark Upper West Side hot spot.
SUSAN (27, long, curly hair) enters. Her
colorful hand-painted shirt and skirt are
conspicuous in this ultra-trendy CROWD.

Susan, shy and always a bit on the nervous
side, looks around and sees MOVIE STARLET
signing an autograph for an ADORING FAN. Movie
Starlet is 25, obligatory dyed blonde, and
behaves as if the world revolves around her.
And it does. At least in this restaurant.

Susan timidly approaches Movie Starlet and
extends her hand. Movie Starlet returns the
gesture with a limp handshake.

                MOVIE STARLET
          Would you like an autograph?
```

                    SUSAN
No thanks. We've already met.

                MOVIE STARLET
We have?

                    SUSAN
Yes. I'm the screenwriter you
hired.

                MOVIE STARLET
        (scrutinizing Susan's outfit)
Oh yeah.

INT. PRIVATE ROOM OF RESTAURANT - LATER THAT NIGHT

Movie Starlet is eating a scrumptious dinner
at one end of a long table. At the other end
of the table, Susan, with no food or drink,
salivates as Movie Star relishes each morsel.

                MOVIE STARLET
        I've been thinking (takes another
        bite)-- about my character.

                    SUSAN
Yes?

                MOVIE STARLET
I think my character needs to
miss the sixties. You know -
peace rallies, bell-bottoms,
gauze shirts.

                    SUSAN
                (respectfully)
That's interesting – but your
character isn't old enough to miss
the sixties. She was born in 1970.

                 MOVIE STARLET
What's your point?

                    SUSAN
Well --

                 MOVIE STARLET
-- I really think she needs to
miss the sixties.

Susan clutches her forehead in defeat.

                    SUSAN
I think I need to get something
to eat.

Movie Starlet takes another bite of her
luscious meal – and takes her time swallowing
and wiping her chin with her cloth napkin
before responding to Susan's request.

                 MOVIE STARLET
Oh. Are you hungry?

                    SUSAN
Well, it's nine-thirty and you
had said this was going to be a
dinner meeting.

MOVIE STARLET
It is. Oh! You want dinner.

Susan looks relieved as Movie Starlet signals
a HOVERING WAITER. Movie Starlet WHISPERS in
waiter's ear.

Waiter whisks off and immediately returns with
two slices of bread and a glass of water.

Susan stares at the bread and water in
disbelief.

INT. MOVIE THEATER - NIGHT (ONE YEAR LATER)

A SMALL AUDIENCE is seated. Susan (wearing a
nice thrift store blue dress) and her friend,
KATE, are nervously WHISPERING. Kate, early
30s, is flighty but sweet, with short-cropped
pink hair and a matching pink miniskirt
outfit.

The lights dim. The film begins. Susan takes a
deep breath.

On the screen, Susan's screenwriting credit
appears.

Susan can hardly contain her elation as Kate
enthusiastically APPLAUDS.

DISSOLVE TO:

Susan is slumping in her seat, wincing at the

screen. Kate, wearing a forced smile, is
trying to appreciate the film.

DISSOLVE TO:

Susan slumps even lower in her seat as she
covers her eyes with her long, curly hair.

On the screen, MOVIE STARLET in disco outfit
is seen overacting.

> MOVIE STARLET
> Hey, man, even though I just told
> you when we were eating granola at
> breakfast that I was born in 1970,
> I still miss the groovy sixties.

In the audience, Susan covers her ears and
GROANS.

EXT. MOVIE THEATER – THAT NIGHT

A CROWD surrounds Movie Starlet, taking turns
congratulating her.

Off to the side, Kate is comforting a
distraught Susan.

> SUSAN
> The only things that I recognized
> were my characters' names.
> Everything was changed! That
> movie was horrendous! My script
> was butchered!

                         KATE
          Well that's a relief. I mean, not
          that it was butchered - but I
          thought you were a better writer
          than that.

                         SUSAN
          Now that's comforting.

                         KATE
          But you still have the
          screenwriting credit. And you got
          to work with a movie star.

                         SUSAN
          But what about my dignity?! This
          is the end. This is going to
          kill my career.

                         KATE
          Don't be all Ms. Doom and Gloom.
          I bet you get great reviews.

EXT. NEW YORK CITY NEWSSTAND - DAY

Torrential rain. Susan, dressed in a yellow
rain slicker, turns pale as she reads aloud
from a copy of Variety.

                         SUSAN
               "The worst film of the decade."

THUNDER. Susan uses the Variety to cover her
head as she runs off.

EXT. NEW YORK CITY OUTDOOR CAFÉ - DAY (TWO
WEEKS LATER)

Susan (casually dressed) is seated at a small
table drinking coffee and watching the PASSERSBY.
Two filled water glasses are on the table.

Kate (purple hair and matching purple outfit)
runs up to Susan's table and grabs a seat.

                    KATE
     I got here as soon as I could.

                    SUSAN
     You'll never believe this. An
     agent called me and requested my
     original script of that groovy
     film. And even read it!

                    KATE
     Even after all those bad reviews?

                    SUSAN
     The agent said that if the film
     got made, there probably was a
     good script in there to start
     with. He also said that he wants
     to represent me!!!

                    KATE
     Vindication!

Susan and Kate pick up their water glasses in
a toast.

CHAPTER
Two

STORY ANALYSTS:
WHO ARE THEY AND
WHAT ARE THEY LOOKING FOR?

WHO ARE THEY?

Many story analysts (also called "readers") are recent college graduates looking to break into the film industry. Many have degrees in literature or film. They are educated, smart, over-worked, and underpaid. Many are aspiring screenwriters themselves who are reading for a company to pay their bills, while others hope to work in development or other film industry positions and are paying their dues while getting a foot in the door.

Story Analysts Are the Lowest People on the Film Industry Totem Pole, but They Are Also the Most Important to You
Despite their dismal pay and low status, story analysts have a

23

huge responsibility – to find that winning property and new writing talent! Story analysts may get three scripts to read overnight after a full day of reading. It's your job to grab their attention and make them want to forward your script to their bosses who have the power to get your movie made. *(See Chapter 3.)*

WHAT ARE THEY LOOKING FOR?

Understanding what story analysts are looking for will help you to deliver a script that they can champion to their bosses. They are looking for a great script, which is discussed in more detail in the next few pages, and they are looking for writing talent.

Story analysts may read a script and love the writing, but reject it because it's not the type of project their company is looking to produce at that time. However, they will file it as a sample of your writing. This sample could get you work on a project the company currently may have in development or on a future assignment. Or the production company, studio, or agency may contact you to see your other scripts.

I'm Tired of Rewriting So I'm Just Going to Submit My Script Now

If you are saying this to yourself – beware! I hear this line constantly repeated by my clients and students. I've also felt this way, but I have managed to muster up my self-control and put my script away for a few days or weeks until I'm ready to get back to rewriting.

If you don't feel your script is ready, then the story analyst won't either. Story analysts read countless scripts per week, so your script must wow them.

The Weigh-In
Sounds like a boxing match, but no. The first thing story analysts do is to place your script in the palm of their hands. If it feels like it weighs more than 120 pages, story analysts will be predisposed not to like it. Why? It means more work for them, and they know from experience that lengthy scripts are rarely good scripts.

Your Goal is to Have the Story Analyst Love Your Script
Story analysts want to like what they read. They all want to find that great script and the next hot talent. Take your time. You do not want to cause any unnecessary stumbling blocks, so do your best work before submitting it. Remember, the competition is brutal!

Story Analysts' Complaints, Observations, and Confessions

During my time as a story analyst for Miramax Films, Punch Productions (Dustin Hoffman's production company), and Viacom, I became friends with other story analysts. We spent our few free minutes griping to one another, bemoaning our fate. We groaned about the often awful scripts we were assigned. We growled over the fact that screenwriters with little or no talent managed to get representation or had strong enough industry connections, which allowed their scripts entrance to our company and into our hands. And then we griped some more about how little money we were earning for being tortured by bad scripts.

During this time, I was asked to write an article for a film magazine about the writing problems story analysts and development executives found in the scripts they were assigned. (It was an easy article to write!) The following is a compilation of my research, as well as my own firsthand experience as a Screenplay Doctor and a former story analyst.

- We are intelligent, but few of us have psychic abilities. If it's not on the page, we have no way of knowing what's in your head and what you intended. (For example: If your characters are divorced when the story opens and this is an integral part of the plot, then establish this up front. Don't keep us guessing unless you intend to reveal this information as a surprise.)
- If your first ten pages don't grab our attention, it will be difficult if not impossible to redeem yourself later. Beware! We could stop reading your script right then and there.
- We want to see characters who are unique, have distinctive personalities, and serve a purpose in the story, otherwise you are truly frustrating us.
- Don't throw in the kitchen sink. Don't confuse us with extraneous characters and plots that don't go anywhere. This is a sign that you are not confident about your story and we know it.
- We may not have gone to medical or law school, but generally we are well read or have personal experience with the subject matter. We will immediately recognize if the terminology or research in your script is weak or implausible. (For example: A character has a prominent scar on his back from having had his gall bladder removed. I have a nice, prominent scar on my stomach so I know this is incorrect.)
- Even superheroes' actions need to be plausible! If you have action scenes, be sure that they are realistic and well executed; otherwise we will be inclined to reject your script. (For example: If your superhero is piloting a plane without fuel and is in flight for twenty-four hours,

we will catch this mistake!)

- If your script jumps forward in time, make sure the reader jumps with you. Whether it's several months or several years, the time frame must be clearly indicated in your script.
- Film, unlike plays or novels, is a visual medium. Endless dialogue and highly detailed description demonstrates to us that you are an inexperienced screenwriter.
- In your description paragraphs, don't telegraph what is about to be seen and/or heard in the dialogue and/or action. (For example: The descriptive paragraph states: Tara will soon find out that her boyfriend will ask her to marry him. Tara is sitting in her living room watching television. Her boyfriend, Ray, arrives with flowers. Tara accepts the flowers as Ray gets down on one knee and proposes.)
- Don't *direct* your script with camera angles. Using camera directions is absolutely frowned upon. We know that directors and producers do not want to be told how to shoot their movie!
- A script is not a novel. Dense paragraphs of descriptions are a turnoff. Each separate action should be a new paragraph. Be brief and concise. Make each word count. Since we are often tired and overworked, these paragraphs become a blur of black lines, and consequently, we may overlook important details.
- Avoid heavy-handed exposition at all costs. Don't over-explain information about back-story in dialogue. We know if you're setting up a whole scene just to get exposition across. (For example: Don't create a scene just to explain that a character has a fear of flying because he once was an air traffic controller. This information can be simply learned in a line or two of dialogue and/or visuals.)

- Watch out for rambling scenes! Generally, one script page equals one minute of screen time. You must keep this in mind if your scenes run long since we are looking for a well-paced screenplay.
- When we read voice-overs, we often panic! We don't want to be spoon-fed information. We don't want to hear the same information in voice-over that will soon be revealed in dialogue, visuals, or action.
- When we read flashbacks, our alarms start to go off! Generally, we frown upon flashbacks because we know flashbacks rarely work on film. If you really feel that you need to use them, know that we will be scrutinizing them to see if they are indeed necessary.
- Incorrect format shows us that you are inexperienced. Don't cheat and use a smaller font or change the margins. We will catch this immediately. Respect the time of the person reading your script.
- Don't submit your script unless it looks perfect! No typos. No coffee stains. No photocopying lines. No missing or extra blank pages within the script. Believe me, you don't want us to become irritated because we are attempting to decipher text between the spots and smudges, and trying to figure out which page belongs where.

OVERNIGHT SCRIPTS

When I was a story analyst for Miramax, I once had six scripts to read overnight. (Why the rush? When production companies and/or studios receive a script from an agent about which there is a "buzz" – meaning it's hot – development executives want to be the first at the gate to make an offer to option the script if they are interested in producing it.) Clearly, I was under pressure to meet my deadline and I was exhausted. Being an empathetic screenwriter, I felt an obligation to give each script a good read. But little annoyances like typos and poor formatting would send me into a tailspin and urge me to reject a script.

Think about me and my exhausted state when you submit a sloppy script. Will I want to eagerly turn every page at 2 a.m., or will I want to toss it aside and get some much-needed sleep?

[CHAPTER THREE]

COVERAGE

WHAT IS COVERAGE?

Story analysts don't just read a script and say yes or no to their superiors – they write a story report known as coverage. Story analysts read and evaluate scripts to decide whether or not the script or screenwriter will be of interest to the company.

Most scripts submitted to production companies and studios by agents, attorneys, or an established industry insider will get coverage. In many cases, only the coverage, not the script, is used by executives to determine if a script is right for their company.

Coverage has a specific format. It contains a log line, synopsis, evaluation, and rating box.

Below Are the Definitions of Each Term:

Log Line: A one-sentence description of your script.

Synopsis: One to two pages that present the major story line and subplot of the script.

Evaluation: The one- to two-page critique of your script will include:

- whether or not your script is appropriate for the company;
- assessment of the writer's competence;
- strengths and weaknesses of characters, story, structure, and dialogue;
- execution, originality, and strength of the story.

COVERAGE CHECKLIST

The checklist below is the last page of a coverage but the first page that an executive reads. (Coverage is usually confidential, and it's rare that you will receive a copy.) Your goal is to have every box checked under EXCELLENT.

RATING	EXCELLENT	GOOD	FAIR	POOR
DIALOGUE	X			
STRUCTURE	X			
PACING	X			
STORY	X			
CHARACTERS	X			
VISUALS	X			

The following items are checked:

Commercial Potential:
Strong:__ Average:__ Weak:__
Audience Appeal:
Mainstream:__ Youth:__ Art-house:__
Genre:
Drama:__ Thriller:__ Comedy:__ Action:__ If other, indicate:__
Recommendation:
READ:__ CONSIDER:__ PASS:__

Definition of Terms for Recommendation:
   Read: Your script has been recommended and will be given to the development executive who will then consider the project for production or as a writing sample for future work within the company.
   Consider: Your script has been recommended, albeit with some hesitation, and is given to the development executive who may or may not consider the project for production or as a writing sample for future work within the company.
   Pass: The company has rejected your script. No one else in the company will read your script.

A Story Analyst Has Checked "READ"...

When a story analyst checks READ on his or her coverage of your script, you've passed the first test. But this is only the first step.

What Happens Next?

Development and production executives employ a varied slate of story analysts with a wide range of tastes and preferences.

Likewise, the executives have affinities for different genres, but they are looking for an unbiased view of a project.

Each studio has its own procedure for determining the fate of your script. The following are two examples of how your script may travel through the ranks from a story analyst to an executive at a major studio:

1. Once a story analyst checks the READ box on his or her coverage, the script will get a second read, often by someone (like the head of development) who selects potential properties for the company to produce. If he or she decides that your script is worth pursuing for production and distribution (as opposed to just being held as a writing sample), it will be given to several other executives for a weekend read. Every weekend, several executives will read the script and meet on Monday to share their opinions on it. If the script is of interest to the studio, they will contact the writer or the writer's agent and a deal will be made.

2. If, for example, your script is submitted to a New York studio office and a story analyst writes an emphatic READ on a script, everyone in the story department will read it. If *they* love it, it will be passed on to a story editor, and (with luck) your great script will finally make its way to the executives. If everyone in the New York office loves the script, it will be sent to Los Angeles and the process repeats, often including starting at the beginning with a story analyst again.

CHAPTER FOUR

IS MY SCRIPT READY FOR SUBMISSION?

Now that you know what story analysts are looking for, you're ready to submit your script. Or are you?

AM I THERE YET?

If you are asking yourself this question because you are having doubts about your script, then most likely you are *not* there yet.

Your Script Is Your Calling Card for the Future

If you feel that a production company or studio will "buy your idea and fix it," do a rewrite. If a company loves your story or idea, but dislikes your writing, you'll probably be pushed off the project and replaced by another writer. Companies do not want to have to pay for rewrites. Remember, your goal is to be the only writer of your project and to receive screen credit.

Yes, Bad Movies Get Made, But...
You are leaving the movie theater and you are stunned. You can't believe how stale the popcorn was, but even more unbelievable was how bad the film was. You ask yourself, "How on earth did this movie get made?!" There could be countless reasons... from too many producers attached to a project with no one in charge ... a weak script that producers incorrectly thought could be "fixed" during the shoot ... unrealistic studio release deadlines... inexperienced financiers dictating the shoot. The list is endless, but the fact that bad movies do get made should not be your excuse for submitting a script that isn't the best it can be.

Get a Second Opinion, and a Third
When seeking feedback, give your script to several people who have knowledge about the film industry and will be honest. Face the tough critique now; otherwise the chances of having your script rejected by an agent, production company, and/or studio are greatly increased. If you are repeatedly hearing the same comments from various sources, it's likely that their criticisms are valid. Listen carefully, and be open to suggestions. This is not the time to be on the defensive. This may be easy to say, but it's hard to do, especially if you have airplane tickets in one hand for your pitch meetings in Los Angeles and your weak script in your other hand.

THE TOUGH QUESTIONS TO ASK
A COLLEAGUE OR INDUSTRY PRO ABOUT YOUR SCRIPT

- Would you recommend that this script be made into a movie? Would you see it in the theater or wait for it to come out on video?

- Does each scene push the story forward and build to a satisfying climax?
- Were the stakes raised as you progressed from scene to scene?
- How would you describe the story?
- How would you define the genre? (For example: Is it a romantic comedy or black comedy?) Was it consistent?
- Are the characters empathetic?
- What were the main characters' conflicts and were they resolved in a satisfying way?
- What were the most and least memorable scenes?
- Were there any irrelevant, puzzling, and/or clichéd scenes?
- Were you bored at any point in the script?
- What were the strengths and weaknesses of the script?
- Were there any holes in the story?
- What surprised you about the script?

Preparing for Your Final Rewrite/Polish

Now that you have feedback on your script, you're ready to do your final rewrite/polish.

Self-indulgence

I refer to this rewriting/polish process as my time to self-indulge. I buy a new CD. I watch films day and night, read scripts, and reread my favorite novels. I sit at restaurants and eavesdrop on conversations, listening for dialogue and stories. I tack up new and inspiring photos or postcards on my corkboard. I even try to take naps so I

```
can dream about my characters. Self-
indulgence is a good thing! It gets me back
into the spirit of writing in a fresh and
relaxed manner.
```

Tips
- Set up your workstation so you're very comfortable.
- Don't feel guilty just thinking about your script. This is part of the writing process.
- Read other published scripts.
- See films in the genre that you're working in. This will help you to determine if the genre of your script is consistent and what the audience's expectations will be.
- Set attainable goals. Some writers think they must write five or even twenty pages a day. Others give themselves unrealistic deadlines for completing their rewrites. Either technique can lead you to submit a script before it's ready and/or create writer's block.

PAYBACK

```
One of my students told me that sometimes
she needs help keeping to her writing
schedule. She said, "I asked my obnoxious
ex-boyfriend for a favor. I told him that I
would pay him twenty dollars for every week
I didn't write. I knew he was such a jerk
that he'd hold me to it and demand the
money. So far, it's working. The truth is -
it's working because I loathe him so much
I'd hate to pay him one cent!"
```

OUTLINES: SILHOUETTING YOUR SCRIPT

Outlines are helpful when fleshing out your first draft, but they should also be done with each major rewrite. Since your story and characters will be changing with each rewrite, so will your outline.

An Outline Will Help You to Answer Some of the Following Major Questions:

- Is my main character's journey clear?
- Where do the scenes drag or ramble?
- Are scenes in the right place?
- Is each scene pushing the story forward?
- Is the subplot overpowering the main plot?
- Are the scenes building to a climax?

Outline Exercise

Think of yourself as a film editor. Here is your chance to step back and see if your script is working. This exercise will enable you to restructure your script by rearranging and/or cutting scenes.

Working with index cards may prove to be the most helpful. Using one index card per scene:

1. Number your scenes.
2. Write one-liners describing the main action of each scene.
3. Indicate which characters are in the scenes.
4. Put the cards on the wall, corkboard, or floor, so you can move scenes around or remove scenes.

SEPARATION ANXIETY

I confess. I used to suffer from separation anxiety. This phobia initially reared its ugly head when I was working on my first spec script. I knew that my script needed to be trimmed and restructured, but I just couldn't get myself to do it. I was too attached to my beloved scenes. I kept hoping against hope that I could get away with keeping them in. But I knew I was fooling myself. The time had come to take action.

I wrote my script outline on index cards. When I was done, I placed all the cards on a corkboard. I was then able to objectively see the scenes that were not really enhancing the story or characters in any way. I then took my next brave step. I removed these scenes and placed them in a folder with the hope that I might be able to use them later on for another script. I learned to feel good about letting go!

GENRE

Genre is the terminology for categorizing a script and/or film. Genre must be consistent throughout your script; otherwise you will lose the reader. Figure out which category your script fits into on the following Genre List. Pick one. And stick to it!

Genre List

(Sample list given to story analysts at production companies and studios)	
Action	Fish out of Water
Action Adventure	Horror
Action Drama	Love Story
Adventure	Martial Arts
Animated Feature	Musical
Biography	Musical Comedy
Black Comedy	Mystery
Buddy Movie	One-Person Show
Comedy	Opera
Coming of Age	Romantic Comedy
Concert	Satire
Crime Drama	Science Fiction
Disaster	Sexploitation
Docu-Drama	Slasher
Documentary	Spoof
Drama	Supernatural
Exploitation	Thriller
Family	War
Fantasy	Western
Film Noir	

CHARACTERS: GETTING TO KNOW YOU

It is your job to know what makes your characters tick. Writing good dialogue is not enough. Writing new scenes is not enough. You must get inside the minds of your characters. You must know your characters' backgrounds inside and out. Knowing what happened to your characters prior to their appearance in the screenplay will help you to define and create memorable characters. When you really know who your characters are, they will help you solidify your story.

Remember, each character must:

- serve a purpose in your script and push the story forward in some aspect;
- be well defined and fleshed out;
- have a unique way of speaking so different characters' dialogue is not interchangeable.

Questions to Ask Yourself about Your Characters
- Are all of my characters unique?
- What is my main character's goal in the story? In Alexander Payne's film *Election,* overachiever Tracy Flick will stop at nothing – she even tears down all of her opponents' posters – to win the student presidential race.
- Are my characters' journeys clear and compelling? For example: Guido's unstoppable mission to save his son is both clear and compelling in Roberto Benigni's *Life is Beautiful.*
- What obstacles must my characters face and overcome? In Nora Ephron's film *Sleepless in Seattle,* Sam's obstacle is overcoming his grief over losing his wife. Annie's obstacle is facing the suspicion that her fiancé may not be right for her.

- What are my characters' conscious and unconscious desires?
- What are my characters' hopes and dreams?
- What do my characters learn in the beginning, middle, and end of the script?
- How do my characters change by the end of the script?
- What are my characters' secrets?
- Do my characters have distinctive physical and emotional traits, ages, appearances, personalities, intelligence, vulnerabilities, emotions, and idiosyncrasies?
- Will an audience be able to identify with my main character(s)?
- Have I given the audience a reason to empathize with my characters? For example: A vulnerable child is harassed by a bully.
- Do my characters have specific attitudes towards each other? For example: In Joel Schumacher's film *Flawless*, two neighbors, Walt, a retired security guard, and Rusty, a street-tough drag queen, are brought together after a series of surprising events. Under their constant sparring and mutual disdain lies a unique respect for each other.
- Do I have a strong antagonist? There's nothing more satisfying to an audience than a fully fleshed-out heavy who is vulnerable, smart, and/or has a sense of humor. In Jonathan Demme's film *Silence of the Lambs*, Hannibal Lecter is an involving nemesis because he's emotionally complex and mysterious.
- Does my main character make a decision that leads to a specific action? (For example: Should I pull the trigger? Should I say yes or no?) Seeing characters make decisions under pressure will reveal their true inner motivations.

- Are my characters active in my script? For example: Characters can right a wrong, manipulate, scheme, and outsmart others.
- What do my characters have to gain or lose?
- Do my characters learn something about themselves that they didn't know before? For example: After a heart-to-heart with her mother, Annie realizes she doesn't feel the magic with her fiancé, Walter, and begins to believe in destiny in Nora Ephron's film *Sleepless in Seattle*.

Minor Characters

Minor characters *must* be as unique and as interesting as your major characters. They can be used to reveal information about major characters, which will help you avoid writing exposition. They can also help to push the main character's story forward.

CHARACTER SQUABBLES

Over the years I've had many clients argue with me about the need to flesh out their minor characters. They think they don't need to waste their time developing minor characters. Not true! If you don't care about your minor characters, your audience won't. And if they don't care about your minor characters, chances are they won't really care too much for your script. Don't be lazy or sell your script short!

Character Bio Exercise

Whether beginning, rewriting, or polishing a script, our natural instinct is to write only new scenes. New scenes are great, but *characters need your full attention.* The best way to get to know your characters well is to write character bios.

1. Write character bios for both your major and minor characters. These can be in the form of a letter, interview, diary, or whatever format enables you to let loose and write! It can be a few paragraphs or as many pages as you need. Try writing these bios in a stream-of-consciousness format. Write whatever comes into your head about your characters without editing yourself.
2. Your characters can confide in you. They can tell you about their secret thoughts about the other characters, their hopes and dreams, likes and dislikes, etc. Have your main characters tell *you* the plot of the script through their eyes.
3. After you complete the bios, look at the structure of your script. You will see if your characters are really working and if your story is solid.

PRACTICE WHAT YOU PREACH

I know that I tend to sound like a broken record when I'm telling clients and students about the importance of character bios. I always get a great deal of satisfaction when they tell me later that I was right - the bios really helped them in fleshing out their characters and story. I'm delighted. I'm thrilled. And then I feel guilty.

If they could only see me at my computer tackling a rewrite. It's not a pretty sight. All that kicking and screaming and procrastinating because I don't want to spend the time writing another set of

```
character bios.
     Once I get over my ridiculous
behavior, I sit down and write my character
bios. My characters become more engaging and
unique, and story problems suddenly seem to
solve themselves. And then I'm delighted.
I'm thrilled. And then the guilt vanishes.
```

Examining Your Story

Every agent and movie executive is looking for a great story. They want to see the innovative ways in which you convey compelling themes, unusual settings, riveting dialogue, and unique and satisfying characters.

How Do I Know If I'm There Yet?
Rewrite your script in short story form. This will help you determine if you do indeed have a clear narrative structure that divides into three acts (a beginning, middle, and end), commanding characters, powerful themes, exceptional settings, and a consistent genre.

Questions to Ask Yourself about Your Story
- Have I put a unique twist on my script? For example: My story is inspired by Shakespeare's *Romeo and Juliet*. Have I expressed a distinctive perspective on young love and family feuds?
- Is my story compelling? Is this a real page-turner?
- Are the stakes clear? What will the characters win or lose? In Tom Tykwer's film *Run Lola Run*, Lola has twenty minutes to find a way to come up with the money to save her boyfriend's life from a trigger-happy thug.
- Is the dramatic clock ticking? Regardless of genre, the

audience must feel a sense of urgency or expectation in each scene. For example: An anxious groom waits along with the restless guests for the bride's arrival. Where is she? Will the bride get to the church on time?

- Do I have a clear subtext? Is my dialogue doing double duty so the audience can read between the lines? For example: A character says one thing, but there's an underlying meaning in what she's saying. Or in action: What is actually occurring as opposed to what seems to be occurring?

- Does my story have the clear three-act structure common to traditional narrative films? (Act I: setup; Act II: conflict; Act III: resolution.)

- Am I overexplaining the story by spelling out everything to the point that I'm hitting the audience over the head?

- Have I mistakenly telegraphed in my description paragraph what is about to happen in the forthcoming dialogue or action?

- Are there unexpected occurrences and conflicts that the protagonist must overcome? In Tom Shadyac's film *Liar Liar*, the protagonist, Fletcher Reid, a fast-talking lawyer and habitual liar, "magically" complies with his son's birthday wish when he must tell the truth for 24 hours.

- Does my story continue to build to a climax?

- Are the ideas that are in my head really on the page?

- Am I conveying and illustrating my story through visuals? *Show*, don't *tell*. Let the audience see clues rather than hearing about them. In *As Good as It Gets* directed by James L. Brooks, Melvin Udall suffers from obsessive-compulsive disorder, which is shown rather than discussed. We see his elaborate routine for washing hands, the way he steps over sidewalk cracks and brings his own silverware to restaurants.

- Do I pay off actions that I have set up? You must deliver

on this or you will not fulfill the audience's expectations. For example: In the opening of your script a character discovers an ancient artifact. (Your setup.) There must be a ramification to this discovery later on in your script. For example: The artifact contains a secret map, which uncovers a major story clue. (Your payoff.)

DIALOGUE

Sparkling, intelligent, and quick-witted dialogue not only helps enhance the characters, but it brings life to your story. Be sure that your characters' voices are not interchangeable. A way to check if your characters have individual voices is to block out your characters' names. Can you tell who's speaking when reading just the dialogue?

FLASHBACKS

Remember that flashbacks are often a red flag for story analysts since this device is often an ineffective shortcut to good storytelling. Occasionally, flashbacks do work successfully, as in Quentin Tarantino's film *Jackie Brown,* where they were an integral part of the story structure and storytelling process.
- Relying on flashbacks to tell your story will often slow down the pacing of your script.
- Try to convey relevant information about the past as best you can in the present.

VOICE-OVERS

Use voice-overs only to convey information about the story and/or character(s) that you absolutely cannot convey in dialogue or in action. Examples of films with powerfully effective voice-overs are *Badlands*, *The Opposite of Sex*, and *American Beauty*. These voice-overs set the tone of the film and got inside the characters' heads in a way that could not have been as effective otherwise.

THE VOICE-OVER GHOSTWRITER

In the mid-80s I was hired as a story analyst for a then small startup company called Miramax Films. Harvey Weinstein was a demanding, yet always respectful boss and mentor who generously allowed me the hands-on experience that I needed to learn the industry ropes.

After working at Miramax for several months, I was asked to ghostwrite voice-over narrations for several completed films that they had purchased from outside companies for distribution. Why did they need a ghostwriter? These acquired films had a name cast and marketing potential, but the stories had big holes in them. Sometimes story questions were raised but never answered, leaving the audience confused. Other times, character motivations were not grounded or realistic to the story. Rather than going to the great expense to reshoot scenes, often the best solution was to simply add a voice-over. It was my job to answer all those story questions, filling in the blanks. In doing so, I would choose a character, get inside

his or her head (by writing numerous
character bios), and then write a narration
addressing these issues.

It was important that the voice-over
have a distinctive style yet remain true to
the character already presented on-screen.
After the written narration was completed,
the actor was called in to a post-production
house to record the voice-over, which would
then be added to the film.

A Variety review praised one of these films
that I had ghostwritten, lauding the unique
spin the voice-over narration had given to
the film.

GRABBING THE READER'S ATTENTION IN YOUR FIRST TEN PAGES

Your script must be engaging from page one, paragraph one.

A JUDGE'S SECRET

In my experience as a script competition
judge, often we are asked to read only the
first ten pages of a script. Given this fact,
be sure that your first ten pages (as well as
the remainder of your script) are gripping.

Questions to Ask Yourself about Your First Ten Pages
- Have I set the stage uniquely? In the first eight minutes
  of the film *Atlantic City,* (directed by Louis Malle,

screenplay by John Guare), a vast amount of information is quickly and succinctly conveyed through visual storytelling: 1) The four main characters are introduced in their distinctive work and home environments; and 2) The unique setting is established as we see the old Atlantic City being demolished to make way for the new Atlantic City.

- Every story begins with the question: What if? Have I posed this question succinctly?
- Does my script open with a gripping event? For example: A wedding, funeral, murder, someone leaving or someone arriving.
- Does my script answer the question: Why is today different from any other day for my main characters?
- Is my story in progress? Will the reader ask: "What's going to happen next?"
- Is it clear who my protagonist is and what his or her need or desire is?
- Is my environment clearly established? Do not set your story in "Any City" unless this is a specific story choice you are making. Characters must relate to their environment, and in turn this must influence the story. For example, setting your script in Atlanta or in a small town in New Mexico will help to define what your story is about and how your characters will relate to this specific environment. If your main character is from Manhattan living in a small rural town in Wisconsin, the character's relationship to the environment should be specific. (For example: How is your gritty New Yorker going to cope with needing to milk a cow in order to survive?) The audience must enter this world with a complete understanding of it.

FORMATTING

Film executives expect you to abide by the strict industry formatting rules and regulations. Be sure that your screenplay is
specific enough so the reader is clear about your intentions.
However, this does not mean that you should dictate camera
angles. This is the director's job and is considered unacceptable in industry standard screenplay formatting.

Periodically, there are minor revisions to industry standard formatting, so even if you have the latest screenplay
software program, contact the WGA for their most current
and specific format guidelines, which you can purchase for a
nominal fee. *(See Appendix B.)*

Basic Formatting Checklist

- Cover page. The script's title should appear centered on
  the page with the writer's name directly underneath.
  Include your agent's name and agency if you have one.
  Include the WGA registration number and copyright
  date centered on the bottom of the page.
- Use three-hole-punch white bond paper.
- Avoid breaking up dialogue between pages.
- Use CAPS for: Slug lines, character headings, charac-
  ters' names when first introduced, sound effects, and
  important clues.
- Use 12 pt. Courier font.
- Single space dialogue and descriptive paragraphs.
- Number all your pages on the top right.
- Don't use scene numbers. Scene numbers are used for
  shooting scripts only.
- Writing "MORE" and "CONTINUED" on the bottom of
  each page is not necessary.
- Brad or brass fasteners are the industry standard. 1½

inches for scripts over 100 pages. 1¼ inches for scripts up to 100 pages.

CHAPTER FIVE

THE QUEST FOR
A WINNING QUERY LETTER

FINDING AND UNLOCKING THE SECRET DOOR

A good query letter is your key to unlocking an executive's door. Writing queries can be a painstaking process. Take your time and be as thoughtful about your query as you were when writing your screenplay.

Query letters must have punch to entice the agent, production company, and/or studio to want to read your screenplay. (As noted in Chapter 9, you may still continue to query production companies, studios, and/or talent once you have an agent.) Your enthusiasm and passion about your project must shine through in your query.

Industry professionals view query letters as a reflection of the writer's screenplay and writing skills. So the assumption will be if the query letter is poor, then the script will be too.

Remember, if you continue to get rejections or no response from your query, there may be a good reason for it. Your query isn't doing the job!

FREQUENTLY ASKED QUESTIONS

How long should the query letter be?
One page only.

What should my query letter include?
It should include a friendly opening paragraph, one paragraph about the project, one paragraph about your background, and one paragraph inviting the agent and/or development executive to read your script. You should also include a self-addressed, stamped envelope (SASE) for the recipient's response.

Where do I find agents, production companies, and/or studios to query?
The WGA publishes the Guild Signatory Agents and Agencies List, which you can purchase. Also, there is the Hollywood Agents and Managers Directory. If you are looking for production companies, one of the most reliable resources is the Hollywood Creative Directory. *(See Appendix B.)*

How do I start the querying process?
1. Develop a marketing plan. If you are looking for an agent, target the Los Angeles and New York agencies first. If you are looking for a production company and/or studio for your project, find out what types of projects they are looking for and what they have produced in the past.
2. Target about twenty companies to start with.

3. Send out the twenty queries and see what type of response you're getting. If you are not getting any positive feedback, then rewrite your query before targeting the next twenty companies on your list.

Should I call every agent, production company, and/or studio on my list prior to sending my query?

Unfortunately the answer is yes if you want results. It's important to know the submission policy of the agency, production company, and/or studio so your query shows your film industry savvy. Certainly this is time consuming and will run up your phone bill, but it's well worth the investment.

Calls will give you the opportunity to make a personal connection to the receptionists and assistants. Keep in mind that today they may be the assistant or receptionist, but tomorrow they may be the agent or executive. A kind letter and/or call may be very welcome to assistants who are often overworked, underpaid, and not appreciated.

If you're looking for representation, you should ask which agent is looking for new writers. If you're calling a production company or studio, you should ask what types of projects they are seeking. Also, you can verify the correct spelling and title of the person you are querying. This is crucial because there is a revolving door of executives in the film industry.

To whom should I address my query?

Address your query to the agent or executive directly, although his or her assistant will probably read it first. If you are querying a production company or studio, do not send your letter to the president of the company; address it to the vice president of development, head of development, or creative executive.

How long will it take to get a response to my queries?
The reply time may be several weeks. If a month passes, you may call and ask if they have received your query and/or send another letter stating that this is your second query. If there is no response, assume that they are not interested and move on to the next person or company on your list. Also, you may not hear back if you have forgotten to include a SASE.

Is it acceptable to fax or e-mail my query?
Most companies prefer a mailed query because they may want to use the SASE to respond and/or enclose a release form if they are interested in reading your script.

Should I enclose a postcard along with my query for a response?
A postcard with a box to check: "Yes, I want to read your script" or "No, I don't want to read your script" is fine, but be sure to enclose a SASE so an agent, production company, and/or studio can send you a release form.

Who reads my query?
Usually an assistant will read the query letter first. If the assistant deems the query to be of interest to the company, he or she will pass it on to the executive. The executive decides whether to ask you to submit a synopsis and/or screenplay.

What if I don't have any film- or writing-related experience?
If you have taken a professional and notable writing or film course, then include this in your query. If you have no experience at all, you may want to state what profession you are in and what inspired you to write a screenplay, although this turns off some executives. Another suggestion is to mention the college you attended or even a hobby you have. This may set you apart from other writers. The person reading your query may have gone to the same college or share your same

hobby, and this will help to establish a personal connection.

How do I know if the production company I am querying is legitimate?

Trust your gut instinct. If the company is new, call or do research to find out whether they have a production deal with a studio and/or some type of financing. You may also inquire what type of experience they have in the film industry.

Do I need a personal recommendation?

A personal recommendation is seen as a confirmation from another industry professional that your script has potential. It also shows that you are savvy and have some connections. But if you don't have any personal connections, don't despair. Writing a winning query will get you in the door.

If I have won a script competition, should I include this in my query?

Yes. If you have won or placed as a finalist in a reputable screenplay contest, definitely include this in your query.

Should I summarize the story of my script by referring to successful films?

Film executives tend to differ as to whether or not a writer should refer to successful films. Some executives want to see that you've written a unique project that has never been seen before, while others like to see how your project will fit into their marketing scheme.

Should I state in my query that I have written other scripts aside from the one that I'm querying them about?

Stating that you've written several scripts is fine, but listing ten or so may be a detriment. The agent or executive may see this as a negative and be concerned that nothing thus far has happened with your other scripts.

If I have already had production companies and/or studios read my script, should I include this in my query to agents?
Some agents feel that this is a positive since you are illustrating initiative, while others feel that you are limiting their playing field with your project if it has already been read. This is your call. Literally. Calling ahead and asking is your best bet.

What if an agent I have queried wants to read my script, but charges a reading fee?
Never pay a reading fee. Agents who are WGA signatories cannot charge a fee. You want an agent who is a signatory because he or she must abide by the WGA rules, which protect writers' interests.

Should I send a synopsis or résumé with my query?
No. Send only your query letter unless you have spoken to the agency, studio, or production company first and they have requested additional material from you. If you do include additional material without being asked for it, this will be seen as unprofessional, and you will risk the query being tossed out.

Should I print out my query on fancy stationery or design a logo?
Most agents and executives prefer a standard, no-frills business letter. They often feel that writers spend too much time on design and not enough time on content. It's the content that's going to win them over in the end!

How do I know if my query is ready to be sent out?
If possible, have it read by an industry professional or someone whose opinion you respect. Ask them if the query was enticing enough for them to want to read your script.

Query Letter Do's

- Be original. Your query must stand out in the crowd. It should show the reader who you are.
- Be brief and to the point. This is a business letter; don't be chatty.
- Express confidence in your work and ability.
- Describe your script in three or four sentences and in the present tense.
- Use short paragraphs.
- Be sure to indicate the genre of your script.
- Provide information about who you are, and any film- or writing-related background. Be honest!
- Enclose an SASE.
- Keep a copy of your query for your files, as well as a list of whom you submit your letters to.
- Always call ahead to confirm that the person you are submitting to is still working in that position and to confirm spellings, titles, and guidelines.

Query Letter Don'ts

- No typos.
- Don't handwrite your letter.
- Don't begin with: To Whom It May Concern. Get the addressee's name and title. Spell it correctly!
- Don't flatter the addressee too much.
- Don't sell yourself short.
- Don't include too much plot description.
- Don't reveal your script's ending.
- Don't beg.
- Don't ask for permission to send your script.
- Don't include casting or box office projections.

Million-Dollar Script

"My script will make 100 million dollars at the box office. I'm confident that Tom Cruise and Madonna will want to play the lead parts. This is the best script that you'll ever read." You may be laughing in disbelief, but these are actual examples of queries that I received from anxious screenwriters when I was working in studio and production company development offices. Yes, your project may make millions of dollars – and even attract Tom Cruise and Madonna to star – and it may be the best script an executive has ever read – but there are no guarantees. Promoting yourself and your project in this way is not a savvy way to grab an executive's attention.

Query Letter Content

Your query letter should stress how your script will meet the executive's needs, not vice versa.

Begging and Pleading

Several years ago I had a very talented client who was diligently working on a screenplay. When the script was ready to submit, she showed me a sample of her query letter. It was an honest assessment of her life, but perhaps too honest.

The letter went something like this:

Dear Company:

    I am married with a four-year-old daughter and am currently working at a sales job. My husband is in graduate school and we are living with his parents to save money. I am under a great deal of pressure to earn a better salary. I love to write and really want to make a living as a screenwriter. If you have some time and have any interest in my story idea, will you consider reading my script?

QUERY LETTER FORMAT

- A query should be in a professional business letter format.
- No fancy fonts.
- Use standard white 20 lb. bond paper.
- Use a standard white #10 business envelope.
- Fold letter in thirds with the addressee's name, title, and address facing up.
- If you have an enclosure, fold the two pages as one.
- The SASE can be folded in thirds.

A QUERY LETTER THAT WORKS

Your name
Address

Date

Executive's name
Executive's title
Address of company

Dear Mr. or Ms. Executive: (use a colon, not comma)

Begin with a friendly greeting and/or attention-grabbing line about your script. Continue with a sentence such as: "I have just completed the feature screenplay [title] that I would like to submit to you for your consideration." If appropriate, include information about why your project may be the right match for their company.

Describe your script in three to four sentences. State the genre, who the main characters are, using their actual names, what their major obstacle is, and how they plan to overcome it. Don't give away the ending.

Give a brief one-paragraph bio stressing your screenwriting or film background. For example: "I am a recent graduate of" or "My credits include: [name films or scripts and awards]." Also, add something unique about yourself that makes you attractive to the production company, studio, or agent.

Closing paragraph. Two simple sentences will do. For example: "Enclosed you will find a self-addressed stamped envelope for your reply. I look forward to hearing from you soon."

Sincerely,
Name
Phone number

CHAPTER SIX

SHARPENING YOUR SYNOPSIS

WHY YOU NEED TO WRITE A SYNOPSIS

Your synopsis is the tool that will prompt an agent, studio, and/or production company to request your script. Why? Executives are inundated with scripts, and a synopsis is a quick way for them to determine if your project may be of interest. Generally, if you get a positive response from your query, the next step may be just a request for your synopsis. Given this, your synopsis must be solid and reflect your talents as a writer.

WISHING ON A STAR

Recently, a development executive from a prominent production company contacted me to see if I had any projects appropriate for them. (It's always a bonus to have an executive call you seeking material rather than vice versa!)

The executive listed the following parameters they were seeking:

- A script that was ready to go. (Meaning that it was a completed script and not in progress.)
- Low or medium budget. (Under 10 million.)
- A strong role for the star. (This production company was set up to produce projects for this well-known male actor, and they were looking for a starring vehicle for him.)
- Character-driven. (No action, sci-fi, or period pieces.)
- Location. (New York City area was preferable.)
- Registered with the WGA.

The executive stated that if I had any scripts that applied, she wanted to read the synopsis and/or synopses. I had three projects I thought might be appropriate, and per her request, I faxed her the three synopses. Within minutes she responded, requesting to read all three scripts. Hence, the moral of the story: Write a sensational synopsis!

Writing a synopsis can also be useful when you are polishing your script. It helps you to determine if your story line is clear and if your main character's journey is compelling.

The process of writing a synopsis can often be more frustrating than rewriting your script. Be patient! It's important to take your time and use that same creative energy as you did when writing your screenplay.

Elation Interrupted

```
You've finished your script and you're
elated! You're ready for the world to see
your script and to start making contacts to
companies and agents. But the last thing you
want to do now is to write a synopsis. I
know. I've been there. And I know what
you're thinking: "How can I convey what my
script is about in only one page?"
        My clients and students always try to
convince me that their "amazing scripts" will
grab an executive's attention, and that
spending so much time writing a strong
synopsis isn't that necessary. Unfortunately,
they're wrong. Yes, writing a synopsis is
grueling work, but it must be done - and
done well.
```

Often my clients will submit a synopsis along with their script and ask me to analyze both. I always read their synopsis first. I am usually quite impressed with the story and style in which these synopses have been written. But when I then read their scripts, I'm often dismayed that they do not reflect the information, style, or story accurately. There are missing plot points, character inconsistencies, but most important, the synopsis fails to convey the tone of the script. (The synopsis may read like a comedy, when the script is really a drama.)

Be sure that your synopsis accurately reflects your script. Ask a few people who haven't read your script to read your synopsis. Ask them what the story is about. If their feedback describes your script, you'll know that you've written an effective synopsis.

Frequently Asked Questions

How long should the synopsis be?
Most agents, production companies, and studios want one page only. Find out specific policies prior to submission.

Can I include a dialogue sample within the synopsis?
If the dialogue sample is brief and will give the reader a fascinating clue to your character(s), then this is acceptable.

Should I describe my character using a movie star's name?
Some executives feel it's best not to describe your character using a movie star's name because it takes away from the originality of your character and/or script. Other executives like to get a clear picture of what you have in mind. For example, "Martin Andrews, a Tom Hanks-type everyman..."

Should I reveal the ending?
No. Your goal is to entice the reader to request your script.

If my script has won a script competition, can I include this?
Yes. You can briefly state the name of the competition and the award you received.

Your Synopsis Should:

- accurately reflect your story and characters;
- illustrate your writing style as well as the style of your script;

- be brief, energetic, and to the point;
- be written in the present tense;
- contain information about genre, setting, and time period;
- clearly set the stage and create the world for the reader;
- stay focused on your main character's journey (keep in mind where your main character is in the beginning, middle, and end of your script – this will help you to streamline your plot);
- illustrate what makes your story and characters unique;
- briefly describe the main plot of the story;
- use clear, concise sentences and active verbs.

Your Synopsis Should Not:

- contain any typos (have a colleague or friend proofread it);
- become caught up in plot details (capture the essence of the story rather than relaying every detail);
- include subplots (these complicate the synopsis and can confuse the reader);
- use a plethora of combined genre terms (for example: "This noir/romantic/comedy/thriller of urban senior citizens is set in the future");
- contain the phrase: "Then what happens next is…";
- reveal your ending.

CHAPTER SEVEN

ALL ABOUT PITCHING

A pitch is exactly what it sounds like – a sales pitch. After all, this is the film *business*. A pitch can be as short as a single sentence or as long as a few paragraphs or more depending on what the executive has requested. Your pitch should summarize your script, entrance your listeners, emotionally move them (make them laugh! make them cry!), and convince them to spend millions of dollars turning your screenplay into a movie.

WHAT TO DO WHEN YOU GET THE CALL TO PITCH

This is the moment that you've been waiting for. You receive the call that an executive wants to meet with you about your spec script. Now what? Panic? Go ahead! Get it out of your system! Then it's time to get down to work!

It's extremely challenging to nail down your entire script intelligently in just a couple of sentences, but it's crucial that you are able to do so. For examples of short pitches, read the inside flaps of book jackets, the backs of video boxes, or summaries of the Best Picture nominees for the Academy Awards (see the "nominees" section at www.oscar.com). *TV Guide* blurbs are less accurate, and I don't recommend using these for inspiration.

Preparing a pitch can serve you well even if you don't have a meeting set up just yet. It will help you to hone in on your story ideas and make sure that your script is succinct. Also, when you call production companies, studios, and/or agents to learn their query submission rules, you never know who's going to pick up the telephone. There's a good chance someone will ask, "So, what's your script about?" You should be prepared to pitch your project to them right then and there.

Don't let opportunities pass you by!

TRAPPED WITHOUT A PITCH

```
You never know with whom you may get stuck
in an elevator. While working as an
assistant in the story department at
Paramount Pictures, I got stuck in an
elevator for a couple of very long minutes
somewhere between the 31st and 32nd floor
with a well-known movie star. It was my
golden opportunity to pitch some of my
script ideas since I had a captive audience
who just asked, "You don't happen to be a
screenwriter by any chance?" The answer was
yes - and I had just completed a new
script. But I was tongue-tied. And I didn't
```

have a pitch prepared. What could have been
a golden opportunity, even if only for
practice, turned into a haunting and
frustrating memory of a blown moment.

FREQUENTLY ASKED QUESTIONS

If I call an agency or production company and get their answering machine, should I pitch my project "after the tone"?
Definitely not. This is unprofessional, and the person receiving the call will press the erase button immediately.

Can I read my pitch during the meeting?
No. Your pitch must be memorized. If you think that you'll freeze up at the meeting, state in a humorous or light fashion that you have a "cheat sheet" (index cards with your written pitch) in your lap for security.

At my pitch meeting, do I need to act out scenes or bring any props?
There are no set rules for pitch meetings. Writers may perform scenes or pitch their projects from their main character's point of view, bring props to illustrate the story, or stay seated and deliver a straightforward pitch. Do what best fits your personality, your ability, and your project.

Prior to your meeting, research the company to learn what the executive responds to, like genre or script styles. Reading trade magazines for stories about other writers' experiences (like being cut off mid-sentence during a pitch) and what they did (kept pitching, walked out, threw a book) will give you some insight. Also, calling the executive's assistant may help you in uncovering some vital information.

Should I include a dialogue sample in my pitch?
If it's brief, and it illustrates a character or story, then give it a try.

Do I need to prepare pitches for additional projects for my meeting?
Having more than one pitch prepared for your additional projects will be a plus. Even if the executive is not interested in the pitch that you have presented, he or she is always looking for new material.

How can I feel empowered and less at the executive's mercy at the meeting?

1. **Be prepared.** Don't use the meeting to figure out your pitch. You must be focused and not distracted.
2. **Be personable.** Make brief small talk to show that you are articulate and confident. This will convey that your project is as intelligent and as interesting as you are.
3. **Take control of the meeting.** You are the one with the great story idea and winning script. You must convey this in your meeting. Get the executive's attention. If you feel that the executive is not listening, speak slowly and quietly. The executive will sit forward in his or her seat, afraid to miss something important. If the executive is rushing the pace of the meeting, seeming impatient or speaking very quickly, you might be able to slow things down. Speak slowly, take some deep breaths, and you may set a calmer tone for the meeting.

PREPARING FOR YOUR PITCH

Prepare pitches of three different lengths: three minutes, fifteen minutes, and thirty minutes. The executive will let you know which one to present. Usually, you will be asked to deliver a three-minute pitch, and if the executive is interested in the project, then you may be asked for a fifteen-minute and then possibly a thirty-minute pitch.

1. **Three-minute pitch:** Discuss genre, basic plot line, major characters and their arcs.
2. **Fifteen-minute pitch:** In addition to number 1, include one subplot and the minor characters and their arcs.
3. **Thirty-minute pitch:** Discuss the whole movie using the most important plot points as your guidepost.

Tips to Help You to Prepare for Your Pitch

- Practice with timers.
- Practice on a friend or, if possible, someone in the film industry. Have your practice audience do obnoxious things, like staring out the window or blowing bubblegum while you're pitching to them.
- Know the company you're pitching to and be sure your project and genre is appropriate for the company. Do your homework beforehand. Call ahead, read the trades, or consult some of the directories listed in Appendix B. Your goal is to find out what types of projects they have produced, their typical budget range, if they want talent attached to the project, etc.
- Whether your script or script idea is fiction or nonfiction, do your *research*. For example, if your script deals with medicine or law, be sure that your plot and dialogue are accurate and plausible.
- If you're going to compare your script to other films, choose films that were successful at the box office.

Seize Your Pitch Meeting

A pitch meeting is essentially a job interview. Be punctual. Appear professional. Be articulate about yourself and your project. Your confidence must be apparent in how you present yourself, not to mention your work!

Tips to Grab the Executive's Attention
- Jump-start your pitch without giving background. For example: "According to the *Daily News,* one out of every three cops is a criminal." Give the back-story later.
- Use brief, but striking visual images or state: "Picture this."
- State up front what makes your story and characters unique.
- Set the stage and create the world for the listener.
- Your pitch should be in the present tense; it makes the story more immediate.
- Use the names of your characters in the pitch. This personalizes the story.
- Each word must be evocative. Use active verbs.
- Get to the point and don't waste your listener's time.
- Don't ramble.
- Be excited and passionate about your project. If your not, they won't be.
- Know your three acts without hesitation.
- Be sure that your main character's conflict is gripping and intriguing.
- Executives want to hear just what your story is *about;* they don't want to hear the whole story.
- You're selling yourself, not only your story. It's like an audition. You must prove to them that you are the best candidate to write the script.
- Bring a treatment and/or script and résumé with you in case they ask for it.
- Remember, a script takes ninety minutes or longer to read, and you have three minutes to pitch and make a great impression.

- After your meeting, drop the executive a thank-you note.

THE YAWN

INT. MAJOR STUDIO OFFICE - DAY

A slick and modern office. Susan enters confidently. She's now 28, hair in a French braid, wearing a simple yet stylish suit.

EXECUTIVE, early 20s, hip and cocky, is CHATTING on a cell phone, leaning back in his chair, feet on his empty and spotless desk. He manages a phony smile without making eye contact and motions for Susan to sit.

Susan takes a seat and waits.

> SUSAN (V.O.)
> I sat and waited for this pitch meeting to start. And waited. And waited. And waited. I tried not to show it, but my confidence was dwindling.

Executive finally hangs up. And starts yawning. And yawning. And yawning.

> SUSAN (V.O.) (CONT'D)
> I felt that I had to take the initiative and seize control of this meeting.

Susan leans forward in her chair and looks the
executive directly in the eyes.

                    SUSAN (CONT'D)
          Worked late last night?

                    EXECUTIVE
          No. (yawn) Lunch.

                    SUSAN
          Lunch?

                    EXECUTIVE
          Had (yawn) a big (yawn) lunch.
          (yawn) Sorry.

                    SUSAN
               (testing the boundaries)
          Liquid lunch?

Finally, the executive makes eye contact.

                    EXECUTIVE
               (perking up)
          If only.

MONTAGE

Susan is calmly and semi-confidently presenting
her first pitch.

MUSIC

Executive is staring at the floor
unsuccessfully fighting yet another yawn.

Susan presents her second pitch. She looks
more confident, gesturing wildly with
enthusiasm.

MUSIC builds to a climax.

Executive is sitting at the edge of his seat,
engrossed. He's almost out of breath with
excitement. No more yawns.

END MONTAGE

                    EXECUTIVE
          Here's the deal. Hated the first
          pitch. Loved the second. Let me
          call your agent while I've got
          you here to get that script.

Executive dials agent's number.

                    SUSAN (V.O.)
          I was thrilled by his response,
          but so drained by the experience
          that I could barely contain my --

Susan lets out a huge yawn.

Psychoanalyzing Movie Executives

Movie executives have reputations for being intimidating and tough. We've all seen them portrayed in movies as nothing less than monsters, and have read in magazines and the industry trades about some of their unscrupulous ways. Don't let these portrayals and stories overwhelm you. Movie executives are people, too, and most don't fit the stereotypes.

- Put yourself in their positions. Their jobs are on the line. You don't know how many pitches they've heard that day. It's not easy being on the receiving end.
- Executives are trained not to react. Even if they love your pitch, they may stare at the floor or tap on the desk, so it's hard to get an accurate reading.
- Executives are eager to discover a new hit, yet at the same time they're conservative and not too willing to part with the company's money.
- Executives know their craft and they know what they are looking for. Your project must fit into their marketing scheme and they must be able to sell your pitch to their bosses.
- The executive is essentially hiring you as the representative to get the financing for your joint project. Look at it this way – your great pitch helps both of you.

What to Expect at Your Meeting

- You don't know how much time you have. You may get caught short. Phones may ring or someone will pop into the office. Don't get flustered!
- Direct your pitch to everyone in the room. If someone walks in during your pitch, include him or her in your pitch as well.

- You might hear: "The part of the pitch that I'm uncomfortable with..." Or: "The part of the pitch that doesn't work for me..." Or: "Where I lost interest was..." Take such comments seriously. You may have had a weak character or a contrived story element. Thank them, and take mental notes on this feedback.
- Once the executive has expressed doubts, that is the end of your pitch. There is no going back once you hear: "I can't sell it."
- If the executive likes your basic idea, he or she may present you with story ideas to help you to modify the script to meet the company's needs.
- The executive is anxious to grasp what your pitch is about. He or she may ask: "Is it a love story? Do the main characters fall in love or not?"
- Remember that the executive wants the audience to identify with your main character.
- The executive may not buy the idea that you're pitching, but may give you the opportunity to pitch another script idea, which could be just what the company is looking for.

Questions an Executive May Ask at Your Pitch Meeting

- Who is your audience? (Meaning: art-house, youth, mainstream, etc.)
- What other films would you compare this to? (Be sure that your comparisons are to successful films.)
- What drew you to this material?
- Who are the secondary characters? What is the subplot? (Be sure that your response provides a clear insight.)
- What do you estimate the budget being? (They're not asking you to give an exact figure. Stating low, medium, or high may be sufficient.)

- Do you have any talent (actors, producers, or director) attached to the project?
- Which actors do you see in the major roles? (They're not asking you to cast the film; they're just trying to get an idea of what's in your head.)

THE BADGE IS ON THE OTHER CHEST

In the mid-eighties two of my short films were shown at the Independent Feature Film Market (IFFM) in New York City. I remember the nerve-wracking wait amongst the crowd of other screenwriters and filmmakers to meet executives. When I finally got my chance, I asked them if it was okay to pitch my project. It was all very civilized.

A few years later I found myself on the other side. I was a buyer for Warner Bros. seeking acquisitions and directing talent at the IFFM. I was given the green buyer's ID badge. I saw it as a badge. Screenwriters and filmmakers saw it as a target. I soon learned that green means go, as in attack. Literally.

Filmmakers and screenwriters zeroed in on me - pointing at my green badge and shouting phrases from their pitches in desperate attempts to snare my attention. I understood their desperation as they fought through a crowd of other filmmakers and screenwriters clamoring for attention from executives and agents - and knowing that this could be their one shot at making contact.

The surge of screenwriters and filmmakers fell into three groups: the underconfident, the misguided, and the overconfident.

The underconfident filmmakers/screenwriters

They would open their pitches with a whole string of apologies seemingly designed to provide me with every excuse I needed not to see their film or read their script. They'd say: "I know that you're not interested in my film or my script, and you probably don't have time and it's not really finished, and I'm not really sure I like it anyhow, but maybe you'll want to come to my screening or read my script." I'd think, no, I think I'll go get a cup of coffee instead.

The misguided filmmakers/screenwriters

They would zero in on my green badge and grab their opportunity – launching into a long and involved pitch without asking me if I would like to hear it. They would keep talking and talking despite the fact that I'd made it clear from their first words that theirs was not a project that Warner Bros. would ever consider. It became embarrassing, like being the subject of a case of mistaken identity.

Maybe I was too polite. I should have firmly interrupted them and said, "You've

got the wrong person. Don't waste your time
or my time pitching to me. You should be
pitching to that person over there who can
really help you. And, in the future, ask
executives if they are interested in hearing
a pitch. If they say yes, make it brief and
exciting."

The overconfident filmmakers/screenwriters

I walked in the door, anxious to get
to a screening on time. The usual surge of
screenwriters and filmmakers approached me -
pressing flyers, inviting me to their
screenings, shouting and interrupting each
other in their clamor for my attention.
Understanding their desperation, I tried to
stop for each one on my way to the
screening room. One guy certainly made a
lasting impression as I was listening to
another filmmaker. He stepped between us,
pushed my hair away from where it
accidentally was covering my green ID badge
and shouted at me that I should be more
accessible. I will always remember him, but
not in the way he wanted me to.

I was even followed into the ladies
room by an eager filmmaker who kept pitching
after I had politely but firmly closed the
stall door. I later learned that, by virtue
of my gender, I was among the lucky ones. A
less-fortunate male buyer told me of an
encounter he had at the urinal. As he
zipped up his fly, a filmmaker approached

him and impulsively asked, "Are you
interested in shorts?"

There are definitely right and wrong
places and times to pitch.

Chapter Eight

Okay, I Finally Finished My Script, Query, Synopsis, and Pitch... Now What?

Congratulations! Take yourself out to dinner and a movie. Better yet, have a friend or loved one take you out to dinner and a movie. Then take a day off and rest, because your work is about to continue.

Put On Your Producer's Cap

The task of getting your script read might seem overwhelming at first and at second and at third, but there is a method to the madness. The secret is to act as your own producer.

You are the best person to represent your script. Even if you have an agent, your agent has other clients and you will still have to do the legwork. You have labored over and lived with your script for months, maybe years. Don't take any chances.

Research

1. **Use an up-to-date resource directory.** Remember, development executives come and go, so someone who's working at a company today may be gone tomorrow. *(See Appendix B.)*

2. **Research companies producing in your genre.**

- Learn the company's submission rules and find out what they're looking for. For example: Querying a major studio or big packaging agency with an experimental narrative art-house script, or querying a boutique agency or an independent producer with limited financial resources with an action script, will most likely be the wrong choice.

- Be sure that your project is appropriate for the studio or production company in terms of budget range.

- Find out if the company expects talent or financing to be attached to your project.

- Learn what other projects the company has produced, either by calling them or researching the trade publications and other resources. *(See Appendix B.)*

- If the company is new and has no credits, ask for references. If none are forthcoming, you do not want to work with this company.

- If a company requires a reading fee, do not send your script.

3. **Read the trades.** *Variety* and the *Hollywood Reporter*, for example, list films in pre-production and development. These suggest the trends that may be "hot." *(See Appendix B.)*

4. **Go to the video store.** Peruse the "New Release" section. Read the backs of video boxes to determine which studio or production companies produced the projects in your genre. Call these companies and ask what types of projects they are currently seeking. Also, contact the

producers or directors with a query letter.

5. **Go to the movies.** Go to films in the genre that you're working in. Contact the producers and directors with a query letter.

TARGETING COMPANIES: THE HIT LIST

Know Whom to Include on Your Hit List

Most writers target only the major studios. Don't limit yourself. Numerous independent production companies produce quality films. Additionally, cable networks like HBO, Showtime, and Lifetime are producing high-caliber projects.

Target Talent

Getting "talent attached" means that you have gotten interest from a director, actor(s), or producer(s) to work on your project. While a letter of interest from "talent" does not insure a firm commitment, it will spark the interest of companies.

This may seem like an arduous process, but start by asking people you know for contacts. You never know where this may lead. If you don't have any personal contacts and you are looking to query actors or directors, contact SAG (Screen Actors Guild) or the DGA (Directors Guild of America) for the names of their agents or managers and send your query letters to those people. Be aware that most agents and managers will shield their clients from first-timers because they want their clients to make money. Often they will consider a project for their client only if there is financing already in place.

Develop a Hit List

It's vital to keep track of the names of your contacts as well as the dates you sent out your material and the responses that you received. It became quite overwhelming for me to stay organized and current. My clients and students also shared this frustration, so I decided it was time to take action. I hired a software developer to create a "HIT LIST" application, which keeps track of your scripts, queries, synopses, and pitch submissions.

The "HIT LIST" allows you to input the following:

1. The names of companies, their addresses, phone and fax numbers, e-mail and Web addresses, along with pertinent information about the companies.
2. The names of people contacted and the people the material was sent to, and any vital (or just very interesting) information about those contacts.
3. The company's response to your material: favorable or pass.
4. Lists expenses.
5. Gives you reminders as to when to follow up with material or phone call.
6. Generates reports and mailing lists.
7. Keeps a record of your pitches, and more.

You can also keep track of your submissions by keeping a notebook with the following basic categories: your script title, company name (production company or agency), receptionist/assistant spoke to, target person, material sent (query, synopsis, script, or pitch), dates, and responses.

The following is a sample screen from the many useful and informative screens available in the "HIT LIST" software. An order form can be found in the back of this book. You can learn more about this software at my Web site: www.savvyscreenwriter.com

"HIT LIST" SPECIALIZED SOFTWARE SAMPLE SCREEN

Hit List - Company View		_ □ X

Contact / Company Hit List
- ▶ Company 1
- Company 2
- Company 3
- Company 4
- Company 5

Projects Associated with Company 1

Target Person

Contact / Company Address

Phone / Fax
- P:
- F:

e-mail / Web Address

Search for Contact / Company Name — Search

Material

	Date Sent	Responses
☐ Query		☐ Favorable ☐ Pass
☐ Synopsis		☐ Favorable ☐ Pass
☐ Treatment		☐ Favorable ☐ Pass
☐ Pitch		☐ Favorable ☐ Pass
☐ Script		☐ Favorable ☐ Pass
☐ Other		☐ Favorable ☐ Pass

Submit Project	My Pitch	Add New Project	Contact's Feedback

Expenses

Competition		Travel	
Shipping		Phone	
Printing		Other	

Add Expenses	History

Contact

Add Contact / Company	Notes Overview	Contact Notes

Project View	Main Menu	Exit

DON'T GET TOO ANXIOUS OR MAKE BLUNDERS

Don't start sending out your script to everyone on your hit list until it has been requested. Agencies, production companies, and studios are inundated with scripts daily, if not hourly. Sending a script without it being requested is unacceptable business etiquette and a sure guarantee that it will be thrown into the circular file. If you don't have an agent, you may be asked to sign a release form. This is a legal document that protects production companies and studios from charges of theft of ideas. *(See Chapter 1.)*

Here's a checklist from the previous chapters listing what you need to remember to do:

- Call the agent and/or company on your hit list to confirm the proper spelling and title of the executive you are querying and their submission guidelines.
- Be prepared with your pitch in the event that an assistant or executive on the other end of the phone line asks you what your script is about.
- If the assistant or executive requests your synopsis and/or script, include a cover letter with your contact information and thank them for their interest.
- If you don't have the opportunity to pitch your project on the telephone, mail your query with a SASE.
- Take a lot of deep breaths and wait patiently for a response. It may be anywhere from two to six weeks or more until you hear from the company.

Hurry Up and Wait

Life couldn't be better! You have just received a response letter in your SASE – or you have just received a phone call from the film executive or agent you queried. The company is interested in your project and has just asked you to send your script to them – immediately.

You write a brilliant cover letter and double-check to make sure your script is clean, and all the pages are there and in order. You run to the post office and make it inside just as they are locking the doors. You overnight your script. You do your own private good-luck ritual dance. Then weeks pass and you don't hear a word from the executive. This appears to be the nature of the business: a frantic frenzy to get your script to the executive, and then the long wait. You are not alone. (I've been there. I'm still there. I've even considered writing a theme song entitled "Hurry Up and Wait.")

It is absolutely acceptable to call or write the agent and/or company to find out the status of your script. You may find that a story analyst has not yet evaluated your script, or that it never arrived to the right department, or that it did arrive but the executive or agent is no longer working there. Usually, your script will have arrived, but checking in will be a positive and gentle reminder that you are awaiting a response.

Don't Be Too Hungry

Don't rush into a relationship with the first person who expresses interest in your work. If an agent or company is interested in you, then you must find out about them.

Common Sense

When I first got into the film business I uncharacteristically lost my common sense. I didn't trust my rational gut instincts. Why? I wanted to write. I wanted to see my scripts made into films. If someone had asked me to jump, I would have asked not only, "How high?" but also, "For how long?" Whether dealing with an independent production company, a studio, or a prospective agent – I was putty in their hands.

I didn't ask questions. I didn't ask production companies if they had financing or talent in place, what their experience in the industry was, or why they thought my

```
project or my writing style was right for
them. I didn't ask agents how they planned
on working with me or how they thought they
could sell my work. The result was that I
worked with people who didn't share my
vision of my work or career. I was hired by
production companies to do writing
assignments without getting everything
spelled out and in writing, and was
represented by agents who wanted me as part
of their stable of writers but didn't really
know how to place my work.
```

NETWORKING KNOW-HOW

You've heard that it's all about who you know. And it's true. The following six tips will help you to become savvier!

1. **Be brave.** Even your most obscure connections to actors, directors, producers, etc., may be a lead. If your neighbor's cousin's sister-in-law is an assistant at a studio, send her a query letter. Don't be shy. Everyone is looking for a good script.
2. **Find work in a film-related field.** Intern, volunteer, or temp at a studio, production company, agency, film festival, or script conference. Even working in some capacity on a student film may open future doors.
3. **Take classes.** Take writing, directing, and/or acting classes with instructors who are in the film industry.
4. **Join writers' groups.** This is a great way to have your work read by others – to get feedback as well as to share resources, stories, and insights about the film business.
5. **Have a script reading.** Setting up an informal or formal reading is a great chance to hear your work. It's also an

opportunity for you to invite agents and film executives (or people who might know them) as a way to get you and your work noticed.

6. **Attend film festivals, film and script markets, seminars, and writers' conferences.** Aside from learning more about the writing process and the film industry, this is a savvy way to share information with other writers and to meet industry professionals.

Navigating Your Way through Script and Film Markets

There are many film and script markets that take place annually. At several of these markets, screenwriters (usually for a fee) can have their scripts listed in the market catalogue and/or placed in the market library for the duration of the event. During this time, interested companies can read your script, or they may request your script after the event is over.

I have been on both sides of the market – as a screenwriter/filmmaker and as an executive seeking material. It can be daunting trying to get executives' attention. Why? There may be hundreds of screenwriters in the room who want to meet the same executives that you have on your hit list. You may be elbowing for space in a mob trying to meet them. Some executives may seem elusive and unavailable. They're very busy and have their own jobs to do. Don't take it personally.

It's important to note that if you have a script in a market library, chances are that the executives will not take the time to read your script there. (It's unlikely that they have two spare minutes, let alone hours to read anything.) If you're lucky, they may take a quick glance at it. This doesn't mean that the executive isn't interested in your work. It just means that they don't have the time.

BEFORE, DURING, AND AFTER THE MARKET TIPS

Before the Market
- **Create an announcement.** Compose a one-page flyer or postcard. If you are on a limited budget, flyers will be less expensive. However, it may be worth the investment to have a postcard printed since executives tend to hold on to these. Your announcement should contain the following:
1. A great pitch. Describe your project in one or two attention-grabbing sentences.
2. A very brief bio highlighting your most important credits.
3. Your contact information while at the market. You can print this information on a sticker so you can use your announcement for other purposes.
4. Your home or office contact information. Include: address, phone number, and fax and/or e-mail if you have it.
5. You can include an eye-catching graphic, but it's the content that is the most important.
6. Send your announcement to the executives you are interested in targeting. Snail mail is preferable. E-mails can be easily deleted and quickly forgotten, and faxes tend to be ignored.

During the Market
1. When meeting an executive be brief and polite. Introduce yourself, state that you have a script at the market, and give them your announcement. Remember that it's the executive's turn to make the next move.
2. Don't stalk the executive. *(See: "The Badge Is on the Other Chest" in Chapter 7.)*

3. Don't pitch your project to an executive unless you are asked to. *(See: "The Badge Is on the Other Chest" in Chapter 7.)*
4. Don't hand an executive a script unless it is requested. Generally, if the executive is interested you will be asked to send it.
5. If executives have mailboxes at the market, putting your announcement in mailboxes is acceptable.
6. Never stuff a script that has not been requested into an executive's mailbox.
7. Don't put query letters into mailboxes. This is seen as unprofessional, and generally your letter will be quickly thrown away. Query letters should be mailed to an executive.
8. Exchange business cards with executives. After the meeting be sure to write a note to yourself on the back of the card to remind you of your conversation. (Trust me, once the market is over it's unlikely that you'll recall exactly what was said to whom.)

After the Market
1. Follow up with an "It was nice to meet you" letter. If you didn't have the opportunity to meet the targeted executive, send a letter introducing yourself and your project; state that you attended that market and regret not having had the opportunity to meet. You can enclose your announcement with this letter.
2. Now, try to relax … if you can!

SCRIPT COMPETITIONS

Winning a competition is another way to get your foot in the door. Listings for script competitions can be found in most film and screenwriting magazines, as well as online film and screenwriting Web sites. *(See Appendix B.)*

Competition winners are often listed in trade publications, and this will certainly grab the industry's attention. Having a winning credit attached to your script will give you the needed edge over the competition.

CURATOR CALLING

Soon after I won first place at a short-film festival, a film curator at the Museum of Modern Art in New York (who was one of the festival's judges) contacted me to acquire that short film for the Museum's permanent collection. This acquisition led to a long-term relationship with MoMA. Several years later, MoMA requested all of my six short films for their archives. Having the MoMA "stamp of approval" opened countless doors to film industry connections, agents, and other film festivals.

Additionally, placing as a finalist in several prestigious screenwriting competitions helped tremendously in getting my scripts to the targeted names on my hit list of companies and talent.

Script Competition Pointers

1. **Read the fine print.** Carefully read and precisely follow the instructions and requirements for each competition, as they differ.
2. **Make sure the competition is legitimate and find out:**
   - Who is sponsoring the competition? For example: Are

they backed by a studio?
- Are any of the judges film industry "names"?
- How long has the competition been in existence?
- Do they list past competition winners?
- Aside from a cash prize, what other incentives are they offering? For example: Will they announce winners in trade publications or submit the winning script to name agents or companies?

Grants, Fellowships, and Artists' Colonies

It's important to seek every possible opportunity to get your work *noticed*. There are many private and government grants and fellowships available for screenwriters. Listings can be found in film and screenwriting magazines. *(See Appendix B.)*

Receiving funding is a win-win situation. It's not only advantageous for your wallet, but it's also an impressive credit to add to your résumé.

Additionally, there are many artists' colonies throughout the country that provide screenwriters with a quiet place to work as well as the opportunity to network with other screenwriters and filmmakers.

CHAPTER NINE

FINDING AN AGENT.
AND HALLELUJAH,
I'VE GOT AN AGENT! NOW WHAT?

Finding an agent is tough and often exasperating work, and may be a full-time job for a while. You may encounter a lot of rejection, but be persistent and don't take it personally. Almost every writer has gone through the same hell. You must feel strongly about your screenplay, and that should be your inspiration to forge ahead.

FREQUENTLY ASKED QUESTIONS

How do I really get an agent?
There's no shortcut: You have to write a great script, query, and synopsis, and prepare a dazzling pitch. Without question, a personal recommendation from an industry professional gives you the edge over the competition, but whether or not

you have industry contacts, you must educate yourself about the business, and you must network.

- **Attend script conferences.** If you do not live in Los Angeles or New York, where meeting agents may be easier because of proximity, you can attend reputable screenwriting conferences where agents are speaking on panels. Try to meet them in person during the conference. Agents who agree to speak on panels know that there are hungry writers out in the audience looking for representation, and often they are open to meeting new writers in order to find that new talent. If you do not get a chance to meet an agent at that conference, then follow up with a letter stating that you attended the conference and would like to have the opportunity to send a synopsis of your project.

- **Read the trades.** *Variety* and the *Hollywood Reporter*, for example, list spec scripts written by new talent that have been optioned or bought by production companies and studios. Often they will list the agent who represented the script. Track these agents and contact them. You must immerse yourself in the business so you'll be well versed.

- **Watch movies.** Track the screenwriters that you respect. Find out who represents them by contacting the WGA, and then query those agents.

- **Network.** Even the most obscure contacts can lead to finding an agent.

MANY DEGREES OF SEPARATION

In the mid-eighties, I went to a party
hosted by film director Yvonne Rainer, who
had been my film instructor from the Whitney
Independent Study Program a few years

earlier. There I met a nice man, a painter, who was wearing jeans and a tee shirt. He complimented me on one of my short films, and happened to mention that his daughter-in-law was the head of development for a then-prominent production company and might be interested in seeing my work. With his urging, I contacted her. We hit it off; she read two of my spec scripts, and she called her good friend (who happened to be the head motion picture agent at a major agency). The agent and I met; he (or more likely one of his story analysts) read my scripts, and he recommended one of the agents from his department to represent me.

Do I pay an agent a reading fee?

Never. A WGA signatory agent is not permitted to charge a reading fee. An agent is permitted to take only ten percent of the fee you receive for a writing assignment or sale of your script.

Is it worthwhile signing with a new agent at a respected agency?

Many screenwriters feel that new agents are hungrier and need to put their names on the map, so it is often to your benefit to have someone who needs to go that extra mile.

Is it important to have more than one script completed?

If you have several finished writing samples, this illustrates to the prospective agent that you are not a one-hit wonder. If you have scripts in different genres, this may also be helpful in order to show your diversity as a writer.

If an agent sends a letter saying that he or she is not interested at this time in my script, but that I should send other material, is this sincere?
Yes. This is a positive sign. Agents are busy and don't have time to waste. An agent may feel that the work you submitted illustrated your talent but was not something they could sell. Send another writing sample!

What are packaging agencies, and should I query them?
A packaging agency represents various talent, not only writers but also above-the-line talent, including directors and actors. They will try to package your project in-house, which means that their goal is to get the team together with people they represent, so in the end they can receive a larger commission. If you have a commercial, mainstream project, then a packaging agency such as CAA, ICM, or William Morris might be the place to go.

The downside of a packaging agency is that often they provide less personal support because their workload is heavier. They also may lose interest in you faster if your script(s) have not been getting any interest and/or if you're not getting writing assignments.

What Agents Actually Do

- Agents seek writing assignments for their clients and sell their clients' spec scripts.
- Agents submit scripts to production companies, studios, and talent, and follow up to make sure that your work is getting read.
- Agents act on your behalf to set up pitch meetings and interviews with production companies and studios.
- Agents negotiate salary and contracts.

- Agents work with writers to plan career objectives and to map out strategies for meeting them.

WHAT TO DO WHEN MEETING
A PROSPECTIVE AGENT

Your first meeting is like a first date. It's important to be punctual, dress appropriately, and be congenial. This may sound obvious, but as on a first date, each of you is assessing the other to see if this is indeed going to be a match.

- Don't be afraid to state your own opinions about the film industry and to talk about other interests. An agent wants to know that you are articulate, can stand up for yourself, and will represent his or her agency well.
- Express what your (reasonable and realistic) expectations are and ask what expectations the agent may have of you. For example: Suggesting your script(s) be sent to five hundred companies per month, and that you *expect* fifty pitch meetings weekly is not reasonable or realistic. Suggesting your script(s) be sent out to at least five or ten companies per month and that you hope to have at least two pitch meetings per month is reasonable and realistic.
- At the end of the meeting, don't overstay your welcome.

YOUR AGENT SHOULD:

- have integrity, a good reputation, and connections in the film industry;
- understand your work, and share your vision and sensibility;
- respond positively to your statement of your expectations.

You are establishing a working relationship with an agent, and it's important that you are comfortable with each other. Trust your instincts to determine if a given agent is the best person to champion your work. This is a business relationship, not a friendship. Don't be afraid to ask questions.

QUESTIONS TO ASK A PROSPECTIVE AGENT

Whom do you represent?
Agents should be forthcoming regarding their client list. Certainly, it's most beneficial if the agent represents clients who are working steadily, as this is a positive reflection on the agent's ability and industry clout.

What type of contacts do you have with other companies and talent?
You want an agent who has established and extensive contacts in the industry in order to increase that agent's opportunities to sell your spec script and/or find you writing assignments.

How many writers does your agency represent, and how many do you represent?
If the ratio of writers to agents is high – more than fifty writers to one agent – question whether this is the right agent/agency for you.

Can I call you weekly or have regular strategy meetings?
Calling or e-mailing an agent once a week and scheduling strategy meetings every few months is a reasonable request.

Will you read my new work? If so, how long should I wait to receive feedback?
You want an agent who will read your new work within one month.

How do agents fit into the query-synopsis-pitch scenario?
You need to prepare a query, synopsis, and pitch whether or not you have an agent. If you do not have an agent, you should send queries to agents/agencies when seeking representation. If an agent is interested in your query, then he or she may request a synopsis of your script as well as the script. Then, if the agent likes your writing, he or she may ask you for a meeting, at which time you may be asked to pitch other story ideas. The pitch meeting will be an important part of the evaluation process, because the agent will need to see how comfortable and professional you are with pitching.

If you do have an agent, get your agent's consent before sending queries out to production companies, studios, and talent. Your agent must know whom you are contacting to avoid overlaps, which would look unprofessional. (Some agents may want to be responsible for making all the contacts, so be sure that you and your agent are clear about this.) Once you have your agent's okay, state in your query that you have agent representation. This will certainly bring more attention to your letter.

Will you contact me prior to turning down an offer from a producer and/or production entity?
This is no secret: The higher the fee you receive for a writing assignment, the higher the agent's commission. Obviously, the agent wants to receive the highest commission possible. However, you may want to work on a project that is personally or artistically satisfying but not particularly high-paying. It's important that an agent always consults with you when an offer is presented so you will have the option to decide whether or not you want to accept the assignment.

The Last to Know

A producer and director whose work I
respected asked me to send a writing sample.
They were looking for a new project to
produce. I had my agent submit my script to
them and then time passed. A lot of time.
Finally, I called my agent to ask the
status of the project. He proudly told me
that an offer to option my script had been
made — but that he had turned it down
because it wasn't enough money. I was livid
that he had not even contacted me. I
frantically called the producer to try to
salvage the project. But it was too late.
They had chosen another script. Soon after,
the producer-director team went on to make
award-winning films, and I asked to be
released from my contract with the agency.
And, my script was never produced.

Hallelujah, I've Got an Agent!

Congratulations! Go out and celebrate! But if you think you
can finally sit back and relax, don't get too comfortable.
Remember, your agent alone doesn't get you work; you and
your work gets you work.

Now What?

- Keep your producer's cap on.
- You are essentially representing the agency every time you
  present your work, so be professional at pitch meetings.

- Agents will expect you to continue writing new and *great* scripts.
- You must continue to network and to make contacts in the industry. Telling these contacts that you have representation will spark their interest.
- Become your agent's agent. You must continue to develop hit lists of talent and companies that you are interested in approaching. Giving this list to your agent will not only illustrate your business savvy, but it also will cut down on your agent's workload, which will be appreciated.
- Be patient. Don't expect to have your spec script sold or get a writing assignment right away. If you're lucky, it may take a few months. Realistically, it takes about a year to get a new writer's work read and into the right hands. Try not to get discouraged.

Chapter Ten

Entertainment Attorneys – a Different Kind of Advocate

Why You May Need an Entertainment Attorney

Here are some possible scenarios for hiring an entertainment attorney:

1. A company wants to option your script, but you don't have an agent to negotiate your contract. Since you need a contract that will protect your best interests, hiring an entertainment attorney will be a wise safeguard.
2. While waiting for a response from prospective agents, you can hire an entertainment attorney to represent you. Entertainment attorneys with strong connections to the film industry may submit scripts on behalf of their clients, and this may be an option for writers

without agent representation. Many Hollywood studios and independent production companies are open to having scripts submitted by entertainment attorneys who are established in the film community.

3. You have agent representation, but you have questions about a pending contract. Although the agency may have an in-house legal counsel, getting an outside opinion from your own entertainment attorney may provide objective insight and best serve your needs.

FREQUENTLY ASKED QUESTIONS

Can I forego seeking agent representation by hiring an entertainment attorney?
Yes, although having an agent may get you more attention if you're just starting out. There are many successful screenwriters who use entertainment attorneys instead of agents. Ultimately, companies are looking for a great script. An entertainment attorney with strong industry connections may be able to cover the same ground as an agent in terms of getting your script read.

Is it important to shop around or should I just hire the first entertainment attorney who wants to work with me?
Definitely shop around. Don't rush into a relationship without being certain that the entertainment attorney has the right experience and connections, and is the right person for you.

What can an entertainment attorney do that an agent cannot?
Entertainment attorneys and agents may both submit scripts on their clients' behalf, negotiate contracts, set up meetings, and so forth. However, entertainment attorneys may produce films whereas agents may not.

How do I find an entertainment attorney?
Trust your instincts and research.

- **Word of mouth.** Ask your friends or colleagues for recommendations.
- **See films.** The closing credits of a film usually list the entertainment attorney(s). If you admire the film and it seems like a good match with your script, contact the law firm.
- **Read the trades.** Entertainment attorneys who have negotiated contracts for screenwriters are often listed in articles in the trades. If the script appears to be in the genre or style that you are working in, contact the law firm.
- **Attend screenwriting conferences and film festivals.** Entertainment attorneys often speak on panels, and this is a good opportunity to see and hear them in action.

WHAT TO LOOK FOR IN AN
ENTERTAINMENT ATTORNEY

- integrity, a good reputation, and film industry connections;
- initiative to get your work read in the industry;
- understanding of your work;
- a positive response to your expectations.

WHAT TO ASK AN
ENTERTAINMENT ATTORNEY

Do you charge for the initial consultation meeting?
Usually this is free, but be sure to find out beforehand so you're not surprised with a bill.

Do you charge a percentage of the sale of my spec script, or do you charge on an hourly basis?
Being charged a percentage rather than an hourly fee may be preferable since you will not have to invest the money up front. However, attorneys want to be compensated for their time, and understandably may not want to agree to this arrangement.

If you negotiate a writing assignment contract, will you charge a percentage of my writing fee or an hourly fee?
As stated above, a percentage may be preferable since you don't have to put out the money without a sale or writing assignment. However, if the contract is considered a straight-forward standard contract, then it may be to your benefit to pay the hourly fee, which may be less than the lawyer's percentage.

What contacts do you have with studios, production companies, producers, and talent?
You want an attorney who has established film industry relationships so your work will be seriously considered.

How many screenwriters do you and the law firm represent?
You want an attorney and/or law firm that has a successful track record representing screenwriters.

Will you assist me in getting my career launched? If so, what is your strategy?
Some attorneys will only submit scripts on the writer's behalf, while others will also provide career strategies, give packaging assistance, target companies, etc.

Will you initiate the contacts with studios, production companies, producers, and talent on my behalf, or do you expect me to do this?
Certainly, it's best if an attorney can initiate these contacts if you

don't have any, but don't be dissuaded from hiring an attorney who will not initiate contacts. Remember, you need to always wear your producer's cap and provide hit lists to attorneys.

Can I call you weekly or have regular strategy meetings?
Unlike agents, attorneys will usually charge an hourly fee for consultations.

Will you read my new work, and if so, how long should I expect to wait to receive feedback?
You want an attorney who reads your new work within one month and, at the very least, gives you general feedback as to whether he or she feels the script is ready for submission and which companies and/or talent to target.

Will you contact me prior to turning down an offer?
This is *your* career; you do not want to be the last to know or miss an opportunity that might best serve you.

THEY LIKE ME! THEY REALLY LIKE ME!
(OR AT LEAST THEY SAY THEY DO)

THE OPTION AGREEMENT
AND DEVELOPMENT DEAL

They like you! They really like you! And why do they like you? You've rewritten your spec script to perfection. You've written an attention-getting query and stunning synopsis. You've delivered the perfect pitch. You've persevered. You didn't give up no matter how many rejections you received. You've networked your little heart out and you've spoken to and met with anyone and everyone connected to the film industry no matter how remote the connection seemed to be. Now, if luck continues to stay on your side, one of two things may happen: *They'll* want to buy *your* script. (Your script will be optioned.) Or, *they'll* want to hire *you* to write a script for them. (You enter into a development deal.)

This is the moment you've been striving for. You're there! You've arrived! Now what?

The Option Agreement

What is an option agreement?
If a company is interested in producing your spec script, its first step will usually be an offer to option your script. An option agreement means that the producer or production entity is buying the exclusive rights to purchase your script within a specified period of time and for a specified price.

How much can I get paid for an option fee?
There is no standard option fee; fees are negotiable. It can be a token fee of a $1,000 or a more substantial fee of $10,000 or more. The amount depends on the type of script (high-concept/mainstream or art-house) and the producer or production entity's economic backing (independent production company or studio.) Often the option price is 10 percent of the purchase price. For example, if your option fee is $5,000 then the purchase price of your script will be $50,000.

If at the end of the option period (which can be anywhere from six to eighteen months depending on the deal) the producer has raised the financing to produce your script, you will receive the balance of $45,000. Or, if the option period ends and no financing has been secured, you keep the initial option fee of $5,000, and you may enter into a new deal with a new producer or production entity.

What is a "Purchase Price," and how much can I expect it to be?
The purchase price is the fee that you will receive for your spec script. Like option fees, purchase prices are negotiable. Generally, the purchase price is between 2 percent and 5

percent of the film's budget.

If you are a member of the WGA or if the producer is signatory to the WGA, then the WGA Basic Agreement for union-mandated minimums applies. The Schedule of Minimums is published by the WGA and can be purchased for a few dollars. If you are not a WGA member, try to negotiate a purchase price comparable to the one WGA members receive.

What happens during the option period?
During the option period the producer or production entity will try to secure financing, attach talent to the film, and possibly arrange domestic and foreign pre-sales. Additionally, you may be asked to do rewrites, which you may or may not be paid for depending on your contract.

Since the producer/production entity now has the exclusive rights to your spec script, you may not have this script optioned by another producer during the option period.

What is an option extension?
In your option agreement there may be a renewal or extension clause, which means that you agree to the producer's right to renew your option for a specified amount of time for an additional payment should the producer need more time to secure financing. Usually the option extension payment is not applied against the purchase price, which means that it is not deducted from the payment you will receive from the sale of your spec script.

What does the term "Exercising the Option" mean?
This means that the ownership rights of your spec script are now being transferred from you, the writer, to the producer/production entity and you are now paid the option fee. (Generally, by the end of the option period, the purchase price of the script is to be paid to the writer.)

Your Option Agreement Contract

Under no circumstances should you negotiate your own contract. If you don't have an agent, hire an experienced entertainment attorney to negotiate your contract. It is definitely worth the investment.

What to Ask For
- **Credit:** Be sure that you are properly credited for your work. If you are a WGA member or the producer/production entity is a WGA signatory, the WGA will determine your credit. Generally, the credit will be the same size on the screen as the director's and will appear before the director's credit in the main titles of the film. Additionally, credits should appear in all advertising and on the DVD and/or video box. If this is not a WGA agreement, then your credit will be negotiated. It is in your best interest to model your contract to the standard WGA guidelines as cited above.
- **Exclusivity:** Your goal is to be the sole screenwriter of the film. Getting exclusivity may be difficult unless you are an established writer, but it's worth negotiating.
- **Rewrites:** There are two main points to consider when negotiating your rewrite fee: 1) Be sure that the expected number of rewrites is clearly stated in your contract; otherwise you may be doing endless rewrites without compensation. 2) Your rewrite fees should be separate from the purchase price; otherwise you will earn less money.
- **Percentage of profits:** It is reasonable for a writer to seek a percentage of the profits. Generally, asking for 2 percent to 5 percent of the net is acceptable. However, it's unlikely that you will ever see any percentage of the profits due to the unfortunate fact that production com-

panies and studios often hide the true profits behind false production expenses – otherwise referred to as "Creative Accounting."

- **Sequels:** You may want to negotiate to write any sequels to your original script. You may ask for the "first right of refusal," which means that you will be the first writer to be offered the job to write the sequel but will have the right to turn down the offer. Additionally, you may negotiate a fee or percentage of the profits from any sequels if you are not the writer.
- **Spin-offs, series episodes, and remakes:** You may negotiate a fee or a percentage for each of these three items.
- **Ancillary rights:** If the film becomes a hit like *Toy Story* or *The Little Mermaid* (usually this applies to kids' films or animated films) then lunch boxes, records, toys, books, etc. will be manufactured, and it's important to negotiate a percentage of the profits from sales of these items.

THE DEVELOPMENT DEAL

What is a Development Deal and how do I get one?
Generally, a producer or production entity, after reading your spec script (as a writing sample) or hearing your outstanding pitch, will offer you a development deal. They will pay you a fee to write a screenplay for them, which they own all rights to.

What does this mean for me?
You are essentially a hired gun, an employee of the producer. It is your job to translate the ideas of the person hiring you onto the page and into a great script. This may be quite a challenge. Ultimately, it is the person hiring you who will make the final script decisions, so remember to be diplomatic when you suggest ideas or try to make changes.

What will the deal comprise?

Writers are usually presented with a step deal. You will be paid in stages against the total purchase price of your script. These stages may include: 1) an advance payment before you begin work; 2) payment for your treatment; 3) payment for a first draft; 4) payment for a second draft, and 5) final payment for a polish. (Often, a writer can negotiate a bonus payment if the film is produced.)

The downside of this deal is that any time during this process you can be eliminated from the project.

Is there really a Development Hell?

Yes, Virginia, there really is a Development Hell, and it is comprised of endless rewrites and changes and tweaks of the script you have been hired to write. What they loved yesterday they hate today. Or a producer's mother just read the new draft and didn't like the main female teen character and thinks this character should be changed to a gay male, senior citizen. You get the picture.

Relax, It's Only a Movie

```
INT. SUSAN'S MANHATTAN APARTMENT - MIDDLE OF
THE NIGHT

A Little Italy railroad flat. Posters cover
the crumbling walls. Papers are strewn across
the floor. Susan, now 29, is pacing in front
of her desk. Wearing pajamas, which resemble a
prison jumpsuit, she has many pencils sticking
out of her hair.

Susan stops pacing, pours the last drops of
old coffee from the coffeepot into her mug.
```

She reads the writing on her mug.

> SUSAN
> "Relax, it's only a movie!" Ha!

Susan quickly downs the thick liquid.

She SLAMS the mug on her desk and sits at her computer.

> SUSAN (CONT'D)
> Inferno! Abyss! Hades! This is my hell! How can I relax!

The phone RINGS. Susan picks up, but before she can even say hello she hears:

> PRODUCER #1 (ON PHONE)
> Susan! I've got it! It's brilliant! It's --

> SUSAN
> -- It's one in the morning.

> PRODUCER #1 (ON PHONE)
> Not in L.A. - listen - the main character should be a flight attendant instead of a doctor. And she doesn't poison her sister; she saves her from a burning building. And I have a new name for her. Ready? Mitzi!

                           SUSAN
          Mitzi?

                    PRODUCER #1 (ON PHONE)
          I knew you'd love it. My
          daughter, the six year old, came
          up with it. Listen, my masseur is
          waiting for me. I am SO in knots
          tonight. Ta-ta.

Susan hangs up and stares at her computer
screen.

                           SUSAN
          I know I should be grateful for
          having a writing job so I can
          finally pay my rent on time and
          even go to the dentist for the
          first time in three years, but —

The phone RINGS. Susan, with a SIGH, picks up
the phone again. What next?

                      SUSAN (CONT'D)
          Hello?

                    PRODUCER #2 (ON PHONE)
          I hope I'm not calling too late,
          but you know the trouble we've
          been having with Maya?

                           SUSAN
          Who?

                    PRODUCER #2 (ON PHONE)
          The main character.

                         SUSAN
          First, she's Paula the animal
          trainer, then she's Mitzi the --

                    PRODUCER #2 (ON PHONE)
          Mitzi? Don't you think she should
          be called Ayla?

                         SUSAN
          Who-la?

                    PRODUCER #2 (ON PHONE)
          Sleep on it. You sound tired.
          Ciao.

Susan hangs up.

                         SUSAN
          These producers can't even agree on
          the name of the main character let
          alone whether she is going to elope
          with her boyfriend or kill him?!

Exasperated, Susan BANGS her head against the
computer monitor. This sends her coffee mug
CRASHING to the floor.

Susan bends down and carefully picks up and
examines a piece of the now chipped written
word from her broken mug. She shakes her head
and reads aloud:

                         SUSAN (CONT'D)
          "Relax."

Susan LAUGHS. She leans back in her chair,
puts her feet on the desk. Takes a deep
relaxing breath - and falls backwards to the
floor.

CHAPTER TWELVE

TIPS ON APPROACHING WRITING ASSIGNMENTS
AND
FINDING HARMONIOUS COLLABORATION

LIFE AS A WRITER-FOR-HIRE

Whether you've been hired to write or rewrite a script, you must understand the director and/or producer's goals for the project:

- Ask what initially inspired the story (was it a news story, a person, a dream?) and thoroughly research all aspects of the material, such as setting and time period.
- If this is a writing assignment, ask specific questions such as: 1) What is the story that you want to tell? 2) Who do you see as the main characters, and what are the major obstacles that they must overcome? 3) What is the genre?
- If this is a rewriting assignment, come to an agreement

as to what *exactly* needs to be done. For example: 1) Do the characters need to be fleshed out? 2) Does the story structure need to be reworked or tightened? 3) Does the dialogue need fine-tuning?

- After these questions are agreed upon, submit an outline or a two- to three-page treatment to confirm that you're literally all on the same page. This will help to avoid future problems.
- Keep the dialogue ongoing and honest with the people who hired you so there will be no surprises on either end.

BETTER THAN SEX

One rewrite assignment I was hired to do required working with the original screenwriter — I'll call him Bob. It was a very sensitive situation. Although Bob was a very talented writer, the producer who hired me felt that they had reached an impasse with the script. The script was essentially "Bob's baby," and I was very aware of my delicate position on the project.

I approached working with Bob the same way I approached my role as the Su-City Pictures East "Screenplay Doctor", and that was to be the objective eye on the project and to inject new and fresh ideas. Bob had lived with the script for several years and knew it backwards and forwards, while I had the advantage of seeing things from a new perspective. As time passed, Bob didn't act threatened by my presence on the project, and he even expressed relief to have me working with him.

On the day we completed the script, we were both ecstatic. The story and character problems were solved and the script was finally working. It was time for Bob to type the final words: "The End." Bob took a deep breath, typed those final two words, leaned back in his seat, exhaled, turned to me, and said, "This is better than sex."

KEYS TO BENDING WITHOUT BREAKING

Co-authoring and collaborating doesn't always match my experience with Bob. It also can be very exasperating if you are not in sync with your writing partner or the person who has hired you.

Put Your Cards on the Table

Doing this from the onset of the collaboration avoids hurt egos and surprises later on.

1. Clearly express your expectations and goals for the script and your collaboration, and ask what the other person's expectations and goals are.
2. Explain your writing process and work habits, and ask what your collaborator's process and work habits are. (For example: Are you a night or day person? Do you want to write each scene together, work separately on different scenes, or work on drafts independently?)

Keep Your Goals in Mind

You want a great script. This sounds obvious, but when ten-

sions run high (almost inevitable at some point in the collaborative process) keep your eye on the prize – the great, finished
script.

Be Willing to Compromise Your Ideas and Listen to Your Partner

Compromising does not mean that you're selling out; it
means that you are open to new ideas. You may discover that
your partner has great ideas and inspiring suggestions that
you never even considered or initially thought were terrible.
Keep the lines of communication open to avoid any conflicts
during this process.

YOUR SCREENWRITING MANTRAS

Congratulations! You are now on your way to becoming a savvy screenwriter, ready to enter the film industry. Here are the three final tips to insure that your journey into this new world is a safe one.

Repeat these – make them your mantras:

Persevere.
Never work for free.
Always get a contract.

PERSEVERE

You have a great screenplay, but you keep hitting brick walls. Don't let this stop you. The competition is extremely tough, but if you believe in your project and are passionate, then you must not give up.

The film industry demands the survival of the most persistent – not necessarily the fittest. This may sound cynical but often it's the truth. There are writers and filmmakers who may not be that talented but position themselves to get the big break. Yes, this is disheartening, but try to turn it around and use it as a powerful incentive to continue to knock on more doors, send out more queries, and drag yourself to yet one more networking event.

NEVER SAY YOU'LL WORK FOR FREE

You might be tempted – maybe a famous director will offer to produce your script "for nothing" or a fledgling production company will offer you your first "big break" in exchange for your script. Don't do it. Working for free is a guaranteed ticket to disaster. You will undoubtedly be taken advantage of. Know your worth. A company should hire you because you are good, not because you are an easy target.

If a producer is very determined to get a film made and hires you because of your talent, then that producer must find a way to pay you a writing fee, even if it's just a token fee. It's not your responsibility to worry about how they will come up with the money. Don't let the producer attempt to instill guilt. Raising money is the producer's job. Your job, and it *is* a job, is to get compensated for your work.

LESSONS LEARNED

I was overcome with joy when I was hired by
an independent producer to adapt a novel for
a screenplay. This was my first assignment.
I was given a contract that the producer

drew up. I did not have an entertainment
attorney review it. (My first mistake.) The
contract stated that I would receive payment
upon first monies received from investors. I
knew no investors were lined up yet, but I
was willing to take the chance. (My second
mistake.) I loved the novel and was so
excited by this opportunity that I accepted
the job. (My third mistake.)

I wanted to be seen as someone who
was diligent and eager to work. And work I
did. I did countless rewrites without
compensation. (My fourth mistake.) The
number of rewrites I would be required to
do was not included in the contract. (My
fifth mistake connected to my first mistake
– the one about not hiring an attorney.)
But, because I wanted to make a good
impression and be part of the team, I
thought this was okay. But it wasn't okay.
Soon the producer saw me as one of those
"expendable writers" and I was pushed off
the job. It was a tough lesson to learn.

Always Get a Contract!

A handshake is only a handshake. If a producer, production
company, and/or talent loves your work but doesn't want to
"ruin the friendship" with legalities, think again, or better still,
run. A contract will keep the friendship intact and protect your
best interests.

Friends and Adversaries

EXT. NEW YORK CITY'S EAST VILLAGE - NIGHT

A bustling street filled with shops,
restaurants, and STREET VENDORS. Susan (now
30, wearing black shirt and black leggings)
and DIRECTOR (50, ex-hippie who still looks,
dresses, and acts the part) are seeking out an
inexpensive restaurant.

                    SUSAN
          I have the contract with me. We
          can talk about it over dinner.

                    DIRECTOR
          Contract?

                    SUSAN
               (fearing the worst)
          The contract that we discussed
          last week. I had my lawyer draw
          it up. He was nice enough to
          barter with me. I did a critique
          of his script and he drew up the
          contract in exchange.

                    DIRECTOR
          That's cool. But, Susan, a
          contract? Contracts aren't my
          bag. I didn't agree to that.

                    SUSAN
          Actually you did when we met last

week. (takes a deep breath) I'm
more comfortable working with a
contract.

                    DIRECTOR
Contracts make friends into
adversaries.

                    SUSAN
I've found that contracts keep
friends - friends.

                    DIRECTOR
You know I'm good for the dough.

                    SUSAN
          (warning bells go off)
I haven't seen any <u>dough</u> yet and
I've worked with you for three
months now and --

                    DIRECTOR
          (interrupting)
I really dig Indian food? How
'bout it?

                    SUSAN
          (frustrated)
Actually, it doesn't agree with
me.

INT. SUSAN'S LIVING ROOM/BEDROOM — THAT NIGHT

A railroad flat in Manhattan's Little Italy.
Susan is lying on her futon, clutching her
stomach with one hand and bills in the other
hand.

Kate (green hair and matching green outfit)
comes in from the kitchen with a cup of tea
and hands it to Susan.

                    SUSAN
          Thanks for coming over and taking
          care of me. (sips tea) Why didn't
          I just stamp "sucker" on my
          forehead?

                    KATE
          How did you know that creep of a
          director had no intention of
          paying you?

                    SUSAN
          I've been working in this
          business long enough to have
          known better. (looks at bills)
          Now, I'm going to have to go
          back to reading six scripts a
          night for the studios to come up
          with this month's rent.

Kate flops down on a nearby chair.

                          KATE
          This is wicked depressing. Tell
          me something positive will come
          from all of this.

Susan holds up her hand as if taking an oath.

                          SUSAN
          I swear I will never work without
          a contract again, and never, I
          mean, never eat Indian food
          again.

                          KATE
          Touché.

They CLINK teacups.

A contract is only good if both parties sign it. If you don't have an agent, then hire an entertainment attorney to draw a contract up for you. If you can't afford an entertainment attorney, there are organizations like Volunteer Lawyers for the Arts that can assist you. (*See Appendix B.*) Never sign a contract without an attorney reviewing it first.

A good contract will enable you to get recourse should a problem arise!

So Sue Me

INT. VOLUNTEER LAWYERS FOR THE ARTS OFFICE — DAY

A modest Manhattan office. Susan, now 31, dressed in a black outfit, is nervously

fidgeting with her hair. Sitting across from
Susan is VLA staff attorney JANE, 35, down-to-
earth, tough. Jane is on the phone while
reviewing Susan's file.

> JANE
> Yes, in a nutshell, the producer
> broke Susan's contract by not
> paying the balance of her writing
> fee by the contractual deadline,
> which was first day of principal
> photography. (beat) Yes. Thanks
> very much.

Jane hangs up the phone.

> SUSAN
> Do you think you can help me?

> JANE
> Yes. You meet our criteria.

> SUSAN
> It's reassuring to know that my
> income was low enough to be
> eligible for VLA's services.

> JANE
> (smiles)
> Well, I believe your status is
> about to change. The A.B. law
> firm has agreed to represent you
> pro bono.

                         SUSAN
          Wow! The A.B. law firm, otherwise
          known as the Amazingly Big law
          firm! They're one of the most
          powerful entertainment law firms
          in New York.

                         JANE
          That's right, and they're as
          furious as I am that your
          contract was not honored. With
          A.B.'s involvement, it just may
          shake up this producer and even,
          dare I say - change his ways!

                         SUSAN
          I like how you think!

Susan rises from her seat and shakes Jane's
hand.

INT. SUSAN'S KITCHEN - TWO DAYS LATER

A railroad flat in Manhattan's Little Italy.
In the center of her kitchen is an old-
fashioned bathtub. In the tub, Susan is
relaxing under the bath bubbles.

The phone RINGS. Susan ignores it. It RINGS
twice more. Curiosity gets the better of her.
She leans over and picks up the receiver from
the nearby table.

                    SUSAN
        Hello?

The bath water SLOSHES.

                    PRODUCER (ON PHONE)
        Susan, is that you? Are you
        underwater?

                    SUSAN
        Yes, it's me --

                    PRODUCER (ON PHONE)
                    (angry)
        -- I can't believe you did this!

                    SUSAN
        Did what?

                    PRODUCER (ON PHONE)
        How could you sue me?

                    SUSAN
                    (smiling)
        How could you not pay me?

                    PRODUCER (ON PHONE)
        But how could you sue me?

                    SUSAN
                    (enjoying the moment)
        But how could you not pay me?

>   PRODUCER (ON PHONE)
>   Susan! How could you sue me?!
>
>   SUSAN
>   (<u>really</u> enjoying this)
>   Thanks for the check. It arrived
>   today.
>
>   PRODUCER (ON PHONE)
>   How did <u>you</u> afford to get the
>   Amazingly Big law firm to
>   represent you?
>
>   SUSAN
>   That was your first mistake. You
>   underestimated me. Never
>   underestimate a screenwriter.

Susan hangs up the phone, smiles, and
submerges herself in the bubbles.

CHAPTER FOURTEEN

EPILOGUE

What excites me the most about screenwriting is the opportunity to bring the stories, themes, and images in my head to life by translating them onto the screen. Having scripts produced has fulfilled my wish: challenging audiences to think and react, and perhaps even making a difference in their lives.

FAMILY TIES

```
It all started when I was a child. When my
parents took me to the movies, I would
insist on staying in the theater to see the
film over and over ... and yes, over again.
It seemed perfectly normal to me. Then they
took me to see the European and experimental
films at the Museum of Modern Art in New
```

York. These films were different from the
ones in our local theater. They had
overlapping stories, poetic language,
amazing color, and astounding images. I was
awe-struck. (I never could have imagined
that many years later my own short films
would be acquired for MoMA's permanent
collection and archives.)

When I was a young teenager, my
parents and I saw Louis Malle's film <u>Lacombe
Lucien</u>. Set in World War II, the story
centers on a Jewish family in hiding. The
film was profoundly meaningful to our family
because one of its stars was Therese Giehse
– my great, great aunt. Like other members
of my family, Giehse narrowly escaped the
Holocaust. (Giehse was a highly regarded
German theater actress – her face even
decorated a German postage stamp several
years ago.)
Before seeing <u>Lacombe Lucien</u>, I had
no aspirations to be a writer or filmmaker,
but I was so inspired and moved, I knew
that writing and filmmaking were somehow
going to be a part of my life. I also knew
that I wanted to meet Louis Malle.
In 1985, I found my opportunity.
Malle was speaking at the screening of his
documentary <u>God's Country</u> at the Carnegie
Hall Cinema in Manhattan. After the event,
he was swarmed with fans. I nervously waited
until the crowd dwindled, and then took my
courage in hand and introduced myself: "I'm

the great, great niece of Therese Giehse and
I always wanted to meet you to tell you how
much your film meant to me." Malle
graciously shook my hand. I then dashed
away. Suddenly, someone grabbed my
shoulders. It was Malle. He asked me to
repeat what I just told him. I did. He then
hugged me and said, "I didn't know Giehse
had any surviving relatives. Are you an
actress?" I was so shy that I could only
shake my head no.

Malle started pounding me with
excited questions: "Where do you live? What
do you do?" I managed to answer, but
barely. Soon, we developed a friendship,
which led to the opportunity to work on his
documentary And the Pursuit of Happiness in
1986. I will never forget when he called me
and asked, "Susan, would you like to work
with me on my film?" He didn't say, "work
for me," and I was very struck by this. And
indeed, the work environment he created was
a team effort. I got hands-on experience
doing research, production coordinating,
interviews, and working with Louis on story
editing the voice-over narration. Louis was
very generous and patient teaching me the
ropes. His patience was only tested with me
in one area, and that was my poor sense of
direction. Inevitably, I would get lost no
matter where I drove with him.

Having a personal connection certainly
was an "in" to the film business, and I
consider working with Louis my first big

```
break. For better or worse the old adage
"It's all about who you know" did apply,
but only to a certain degree. Had I not had
the experience making my six short films and
working at several companies, including
Paramount Pictures, it's very unlikely that
Louis would have hired me purely based on
my family lineage. I still had to prove to
myself and to Louis that I could do a good
job.
```

After almost twenty years of working in various capacities in the film industry, I still hold onto my belief in the power of movies. Movies can influence and provoke, and become part of the cultural language. Movies can even change the way we see the world. It is a profound responsibility to have the opportunity to communicate ideas to an audience. We screenwriters *can* make a difference. You can make a difference. Good luck!

APPENDIX
A

SAVVY LINGO
(GLOSSARY OF SCREENPLAY AND FILM TERMS)

Appendix
A

Savvy Lingo
(Glossary of Screenplay and Film Terms)

A-LIST: Talent/star who can potentially draw big box office and/or get a project made by just having his or her name attached.

ABOVE-THE-LINE: A term describing budget fees for story, screenplay, producer(s), director, and cast.

ADAPTATION: A screenplay based on another source, such as a novel, short story, magazine or newspaper article.

AGENT: A person who represents clients, negotiates contracts on their behalf, and is state-licensed.

ASSOCIATE PRODUCER: A free-for-all! The definition of this credit varies depending on the individual's role on the film. It can be given to the person working under the producer, sharing in the creative and business duties, to a financier, or even to a person who brought the script or property to the producer.

ATTACHMENTS: Actors, director, and/or producers who agree to work on a film. These "name" attachments will often help to get a film financed and/or produced.

B-LIST: Talent and/or stars who are considered second tier in terms of drawing big box office.

BACK END: The percentage of a film's profits contractually paid to name talent after the film is released.

BEAT: A single dramatic moment or a single dramatic event in a screenplay.

BELOW-THE-LINE: A term referring to those budget costs for production and post-production, including technicians, materials, and labor.

BOFFO: A slang word often used in the Hollywood trades meaning huge box office receipts.

BOMB: The opposite of boffo, meaning poor box office receipts.

BUDGET: The financial breakdown of specific expenditures to produce a film.

BUZZ: What everyone in the film business is talking about – a hot project or talent considered to have enormous box office potential.

CASTING DIRECTOR: The person or company who auditions, negotiates contracts, and hires the actors for a film. A casting director reports to the director and/or producer of the film.

CHARACTER ARC: The terminology most commonly used to describe a character's development from the beginning to the end of the script.

DEAL BREAKER: Term(s) of a contract negotiation that cannot be agreed upon, which can result in ending the negotiations.

DEAL MEMO: A fully and legally binding written agreement stating the terms of the forthcoming legal contract.

DEVELOPMENT: The process of developing a script or idea with the goal being a script ready for production.

DEVELOPMENT DEAL: An agreement in which a writer is hired by a production company or studio to work on the script, starting either from the idea stage or first-draft stage, and proceeding through several rewrites.

DEVELOPMENT HELL: What you want to avoid! The unenviable situation of being hired to develop a screenplay and having to write endless revisions without proper compensation.

DIRECT TO VIDEO: A feature film that does not get released theatrically and is only released on home video.

DIRECTOR OF DEVELOPMENT or DEVELOPMENT EXECUTIVE: The person who oversees the development of a script and finds new material for the company to produce.

DISTRIBUTOR: The studio or distribution company that supplies the prints to the theaters, and books the theaters for the film's release.

ELEMENTS: Talent (actors, directors, etc.) who agree to work on the film.

END CREDITS: The cast and crew credits that are seen at the end of the film. Contracts will include specifications of the size of the credit and placement on the screen.

EXECUTIVE PRODUCER: The person who either finances or secures the financing for a film.

EXPLOITATION FILM: A film that contains gratuitous sex and violence.

EXPOSITION: Back-story or facts about the story or character.

FEATURE: A film whose length is approximately two hours.

FILM NOIR: A film genre wherein the story and characters are regarded as dark and mysterious. *Double Indemnity* is an example of a classic film noir.

FINANCIER: An individual or studio that invests money to produce a film.

FLASHBACKS: Scenes that jump back in time to illustrate the history of a character or story. Flashbacks should be used with caution.

GREEN LIGHT: Green means Go! A term describing a script that has been approved for production.

GROSS: The total box office earnings that a film has generated. This may also include video rentals and licensing fees.

HARD-SELL: A script or idea that is considered non-commercial and/or difficult to sell.

HIGH CONCEPT: A script or story idea that is considered extremely commercial. Also may be defined as a story idea that is conveyed in one powerful sentence.

INDEPENDENT PRODUCER: A producer who develops material and finds financing for a project without being under contract with a studio.

INDEPENDENT PRODUCTION: A film that is not studio financed. However, a studio may distribute a film that was independently produced.

IN THE CAN: A term used to describe a filmed scene or a film that has completed principal photography.

LIMITED RELEASE: 1) A completed film (such as an art or foreign film) that is marketed and screened to a targeted audience because of its specialized appeal. 2) A completed film that is first shown to small audiences to test-market their interest and may later be distributed in wider release (to more theaters).

LINE PRODUCER: The person who supervises above-the-line and below-the-line elements during production.

LOG LINE: A one- or two-sentence synopsis of a script.

LOOP: The process of re-recording or adding new dialogue or additional sounds in post-production.

LOW BUDGET: A feature film produced for significantly less money than a Hollywood studio film.

MINIMUM: The lowest fee a writer may receive under the Writers Guild Minimum Basic Agreement.

MONTAGE: A series of short scenes that occurs over a period of hours, days, months, or years.

NEGATIVE PICK-UP: The deal between a producer and a distributor who pays a fee for the rights to distribute the film. The fee is usually paid to the producer upon delivery of the film's cut negative. Many films are either partially or fully financed in this manner.

NET: The percentage of the film's profits, which is determined after production costs, prints and advertising, etc. are deducted. The term "Creative Accounting" is often used when defining this term.

NO BUDGET: A film produced for significantly less money than a low-budget film. (Terms like "beg, borrow, steal, and max out one's credit cards" are associated with this definition.)

NON-THEATRICAL: A film that is not distributed in theaters. Examples: television, videos, cable, schools, and libraries.

OFF CAMERA (OC): A term meaning an action that is referred to, but not seen on camera.

OFF SCREEN (OS): A term that refers to a sound or action that is heard, but is not seen on film.

ON CAMERA: A term that refers to an actor or object that is seen by the camera and is filmed.

OPTION: The fee a writer is paid for exclusive rights for his or her script for a specified period of time.

ORIGINAL SCREENPLAY: A screenplay that is not adapted from another source, such as a novel or play.

PACING: A term referring to the rhythm and timing of the dialogue or action in each scene or in the entire script.

PACKAGE: The various elements and/or talent agents bring together to sell a project. The more talent the agent/agency packages in-house, the higher their total fee will be.

PASS: Term used when a story analyst, agent, or producer rejects material.

PAY OR PLAY: A contractual term meaning that an employer (for example: producer) must pay the employee (for example: talent) regardless of whether services are performed.

POINTS: The percentage of net or gross profits of a film. Talent (writers, actors, directors, producers) may negotiate as part of their contract to receive points in addition to or instead of their fee. Gross points are the most beneficial.

POST-PRODUCTION: Processes that occur after a film is shot. These include editing, looping, music scoring, opticals, and mixing.

PRE-PRODUCTION: The preparation for the filming of a script. This includes fine-tuning of the script, hiring the cast and crew, preparing a script breakdown and budget, set construction, costume design, and location scouting.

PREMISE: The basic idea of the script's story.

PRINCIPAL PHOTOGRAPHY: The commencement of filming of the completed script.

PRINCIPAL PLAYERS: The main actors in the film.

PRODUCER: A person who finds material, develops scripts, hires talent, raises financing, and/or oversees the production of a film.

PRODUCTION ASSISTANT: A person who works in an entry-level position on a film production crew.

PRODUCTION COMPANY: The entity responsible for the development and production of a film.

PROFITS: The net and/or gross profits of a film.

PROJECTION: Producers or industry professionals' forecast of the hoped-for earnings of a film. These projections are often covered in the trades.

PROPERTY: A term used to describe a script or other literary material.

PUBLIC DOMAIN: Material or property (such as a novel) available for the public's use to be adapted without a fee because the copyright has expired or was not necessary.

RELEASE FORM: A legal document that protects a studio or a production company from charges of plagiarism or theft.

REMAKE: A new film based on an existing film.

SCALE: The minimum WGA payment based on the film's budget status (low, medium, or high).

SCREENPLAY BY: The credit given to the writer or writers of a screenplay.

SELL-THROUGH: A film that is produced specifically to be released for sale, but not rental, to the home video market.

SEQUEL: A film that is a follow-up to an existing film. (Examples: The Rocky, Austin Powers, and James Bond films.)

SHARED CARD: An on-screen credit where more than one talent's name appears.

SHOOTING SCRIPT: The final draft of a screenplay; the one that will be filmed and includes the director's camera direction and notes.

SINGLE CARD: An on-screen credit where the name of only one talent appears.

SOLICITED: A script submitted by an agent.

SPEC: A screenplay written on speculation (no payment) with the goal of selling, or a screenplay written before a deal is negotiated.

SPINE: Terminology used to describe the critical events in a story.

STABLE: An agent or agency's roster of clients.

STAGED READING: The live performance of a screenplay by actors.

STORY EDITOR: A person who supervises story analysts, reviews their coverage, and forwards promising material to their superiors.

STORYBOARD: A series of drawings placed in sequential order to illustrate the progression of shots in a film. Generally, only action or special-effects sequences are storyboarded since they are difficult and/or expensive to shoot.

STUDIO: A production company that develops, produces, and distributes major motion pictures and network television shows.

TAKE A MEETING: A slang expression meaning to have a meeting. Another common colloquialism with a similar meaning is: "Do Lunch."

TITLES: The printed words at the beginning and end of a film. The film's title is known as the main title.

THREE-ACT STRUCTURE: The structure commonly used in traditional narrative films. Act I: setup; Act II: conflict; Act III: resolution.

TRADES/TRADE PAPERS: Daily and weekly newspapers or magazines that specialize in the news of the entertainment industry, i.e. the *Hollywood Reporter* and *Variety*.

TRAILER: A synopsized version of a film; a few minutes long, it is used as a coming attraction to entice an audience to see the entire film.

TREATMENT: The prose version of a screenplay.

TURNAROUND: A script that is no longer in active development at a studio and is offered for sale to other studios or entities.

UNSOLICITED: A script that is not represented by an agent.

VOICE-OVER: The narration heard off-screen and over what is seen on film. It can describe past history of the character(s), the story, and/or setting.

WORK-FOR-HIRE: Opposite of a spec script. A screenplay and/or treatment that a screenwriter has been paid to write. Generally, the rights of this work will be owned by the producer/company.

APPENDIX
B

CineFile
(Print and Online Resources)

APPENDIX
B

CineFile
(Print and Online Resources)

Updated listings of the following resources complete with hyperlinks can be found at:

www.savvyscreenwriter.com

The following resources are listings, not endorsements. Parenthetical descriptions of resources are a *brief* overview, and most offer additional services.

TRADE PUBLICATIONS

Creative Screenwriting: 6404 Hollywood Boulevard, Suite 415, Los Angeles, CA 90028. Phone: (323) 957-1405.
Web site: www.creativescreenwriting.com (industry articles)

Fade In Magazine: 289 South Robertson Boulevard, Suite 465, Beverly Hills, CA 90211.
Web site: www.fadeinmag.com (lists script competitions, industry articles)

Film Comment Magazine: 70 Lincoln Center Plaza, 4th Floor, New York, NY 10023. Phone: (888) 313-6085.
Web site: www.filmlinc.com (industry articles)

Filmmaker Magazine: 110 West 57th Street, New York, NY 10019. Phone: (212) 581-8080 or (800) FILMMAG.
Web site: www.filmmag.com (lists script competitions, conferences, workshops, industry articles)

The Hollywood Reporter: 5055 Wilshire Boulevard, Los Angeles, CA 90036-4396. Phone: (323) 525-2150.
Web site: www.hollywoodreporter.com (industry articles)

Hollywood Scriptwriter: P.O. Box 10277, Burbank, CA 91510.
Phone: (818) 845-5525.
Web site: www.hollywoodscriptwriter.com (industry articles)

The Independent Film & Video Monthly: 304 Hudson Street, 6th floor, New York, NY 10013. Phone: (212) 807-1400.
Web site: www.aivf.org (lists competitions, seminars, resources & opportunities, industry articles)

indieWIRE: 110 West 57th Street, 3rd floor, New York, NY 10019-3319. Phone: (212) 581-7642.
Web site: www.indieWIRE.com (multi-platform film magazine available online, on newsstands, and in theaters: industry articles)

Inside Film Online: 8421 Wilshire Boulevard, 3rd floor, Beverly Hills, CA 90211.
Web site: www.insidefilm.com (lists conferences, script competitions, industry articles)

Moviebytes: c/o Frederick Mensch Multimedia, 254 South Greenwood Avenue, Palatine, IL 60067. Phone: (847) 776-0747.
Web site: www.moviebytes.com (online publication lists screenwriting competitions, resources, industry articles)

MovieMaker Magazine: 2265 Westwood Boulevard, Mailbox #479, Los Angeles, CA 90064. Phone: (888) 625-3668.
Web site: www.moviemaker.com (available online and on newsstands: industry articles)

newenglandfilm.com: P.O. Box 1195, Boston, MA 02117. Phone: (781) 756-0294.
Web site: www.newenglandfilm.com (online film magazine lists screenplay competitions, resources, industry articles)

The New York Screenwriter Monthly: 655 Fulton Street, Suite 276, Brooklyn, NY 11217. Phone: (718) 398-7197 ext. 2.
Web site: www.nyscreenwriter.com (lists agents and companies seeking material, screenplay competitions, conferences, seminars, industry articles)

Premiere Magazine: Phone: (800) 289-2489.
Web site: www.premieremag.com (industry articles)

Scenario: The Magazine of Screenwriting Art: 3200 Tower Oaks Boulevard, Rockville, MD 20852. Phone: (800) 222-2654. Web site: www.scenariomag.com (publishes complete scripts and industry articles)

ScreenTalk:
Web site: www.screentalk.org (online international screenwriting publication: industry articles, published scripts)

Screenwriters Online Insider Report: 16752 Bollinger Drive, Pacific Palisades, CA 90272.
Web site: www.screenwriter.com (industry articles)

Screenwriters Utopia:
Web site: www.screenwritersutopia.com (online screenwriting magazine lists competitions, seminars, industry articles)

Scr(i)pt Magazine: 5638 Sweet Air Road, Baldwin, MD 21013. Phone: (888) 287-0932.
Web site: www.scriptmag.com (industry articles)

Variety: (Daily and Weekly) 5700 Wilshire Boulevard, Suite 120, Los Angeles, CA 90036. Or 245 West 17th Street, New York, NY 10011. (800) 323-4345.
Web site: www.variety.com (industry articles)

Wordplay:
Web site: www.wordplayer.com (online screenwriting magazine: industry articles)

Writer's Digest: 1507 Dana Avenue, Cincinnati, OH 45207. Phone: (513) 531-2222.
Web site: www.writersdigest.com (lists script competitions, seminars, industry articles)

Written By: Writers Guild of America, West, 7000 West Third Street, Los Angeles, CA 90048. Phone: (888) 974-8629.
Web site: www.wga.org (monthly publication of the WGA West: industry articles)

ORGANIZATIONS

Academy of Motion Picture Arts & Sciences: 8949 Wilshire Boulevard, Beverly Hills, CA 90211-1972. Phone: (310) 247-3000.
Web site: www.oscars.org (sponsors the Academy Awards, educational programs, seminars, Nicholl fellowships)

Academy of Television Arts & Sciences: 5220 Lankershim Boulevard, North Hollywood, CA 91601. Phone: (818) 754-2800.
Web site: www.emmys.org (education programs)

American Film Institute: 2021 North Western Avenue, Los Angeles, CA 90027. Phone: (323) 856-7600.
Web site: www.afionline.org (school, seminars)

American Screenwriters Association: P.O. Box 12860, Cincinnati, OH 45212. Phone: (513) 731-9212.
Web site: www.asascreenwriters.com (nationwide chapters & affiliates: newsletter, conferences, resources, competitions)

Association of Independent Video and Filmmakers: 304 Hudson Street, 6th floor, New York, NY 10013. Phone: (212) 807-1400.
Web site: www.aivf.org (workshops, publications, resources, facilities)

Boston Film and Video Foundation: 1126 Boylston Street, Boston, MA 02215. Phone: (617) 536-1540.
Web site: www.bfvf.org (seminars, workshops, production facilities)

Cinestory: University of Chicago, Gleacher Center, Suite 36, 450 North Cityfront Plaza Drive, Chicago, IL 60611. Phone: (312) 464-8725 or: (800) 6-STORY6.
Web site: www.cinestory.com (sponsors Cinestory Screenwriting Awards, workshops, seminars)

Directors Guild of America East: 110 West 57th Street, New York, NY 10019. Phone: (212) 581-0370.
Web site: www.dga.org

Directors Guild of America West: 7920 Sunset Boulevard, Los Angeles, CA 90046. Phone: (310) 289-2000.
Web site: www.dga.org (publishes DGA Magazine: industry articles)

Dramatists Guild of America: 1501 Broadway, Suite 701, New York, NY 10036. Phone: (212) 398-9366.
Web site: www.dramaguild.com (seminars)

The Fifth Night at the Nuyorican Poets Café: P.O. Box 20328, Tompkins Square Station, New York, NY 10009. Phone: (212) 529-9329.
Web site: www.nuyorican.com (screenplay readings, screenings)

Film Arts Foundation: 346 Ninth Street, 2nd floor, San Francisco, CA 94103. Phone: (415) 552-8760.
Web site: www.filmarts.org (seminars, screenings, resources for independent filmmakers)

Filmmakers Collaborative: 29 Greene Street, New York, NY 10013. Phone: (212) 966-3030.
Web site: www.filmmakers.org (facilities for independent filmmakers, seminars through The Reel School)

Film/Video Arts: 50 Broadway, 21st floor, New York, NY 10004. Phone: (212) 673-9361.
Web site: www.fva.com (equipment rental, seminars, workshops)

The Foundation Center: 79 Fifth Avenue, New York, NY 10003. Phone: (212) 620-4230.
Web site: www.fndcenter.org (locations also in Atlanta, Cleveland, San Francisco, and Washington, DC: resource center(s) and online information for grants, workshops)

Grub Street Writers: 265 Willow Street, Somerville, MA 02144. Phone: (617) 623-8100.
Web site: www.grubstreet.com (seminars, workshops)

Independent Feature Project/East: 104 West 29th Street, 12th floor, New York, NY 10001. Phone: (212) 465-8200.
Web site: www.ifp.org (sponsors the Independent Feature Film Market, seminars, screenings, and other resources, including the IFP/Midwest in Chicago, and IFP/South in Miami)

Independent Feature Project/West: 1964 Westwood
Boulevard, Suite 205, Los Angeles, CA 90025. Phone: (310)
475-4379.
Web site: www.ifpwest.org (sponsors the Independent Spirit
Awards, seminars, screenings, producer series, and other
resources)

New York Women in Film and Television: 6 East 39th Street,
12th floor, New York, NY 10016. Phone: (212) 679-0870.
Web site: www.nywift.org (seminars, screenings)

Northwest Screenwriters' Guild: 4756 University Village
Place NE, Suite 439, Seattle, WA 98105. Phone: (206) 517-
7880.
Web site: www.nwsg.org (workshops, readings, events)

The Organization of Black Screenwriters, Inc.: P.O. Box
70160, Los Angeles, CA 90070-0160. Phone: (323) 882-4166.
Web site: www.obswriter.com (script competitions, script
development, agent outreach, events)

Philadelphia Volunteer Lawyers for the Arts: 251 South 8th
Street, Philadelphia, PA 19103. Phone: (215) 545-3385.
Web site: www.libertynet.org/pvla (their Web site lists contact
information for VLA offices throughout the country)

Producers Guild of America: 6363 Sunset Boulevard, 9th
floor, Los Angeles, CA 90028. Phone: (323) 960-2590.
Web site: www.producersguild.com (publishes POV online
magazine, resources)

Screen Actors Guild (National Office): 5757 Wilshire Boulevard,
Los Angeles, CA 90036-3600. Phone: (323) 954-1600.
Web site: www.sag.com (resources)

Screen Actors Guild (NY): 1515 Broadway, 44th floor, New York, NY 10036. Phone: (212) 944-1030.
Web site: www.sag.com (resources)

The Sundance Institute: 8857 West Olympic Boulevard, Beverly Hills, CA 90211. Phone: (310) 360-1981.
Web site: www.sundance.org (sponsors Sundance Film Festival, writers fellowship program, events)

U.S. Copyright Office: Library of Congress, 101 Independence Avenue, S.E., Washington, DC 20559. Phone: (202) 707-9100.
Web site: www.loc.gov/copyright (for application forms)

Volunteer Lawyers for the Arts: 1 East 53rd Street, 6th floor, New York, NY 10022. Phone: (212) 319-2787.
(assists artists in need, seminars)

Women in Film: 6464 Sunset Boulevard, Suite 1080, Hollywood, CA 90028. Phone: (323) 463-6040.
Web site: www.wif.org (seminars, screenings)

Women in Film & Video New England: 13 Mooney Street, Cambridge, MA 02138. Phone: (617) 491-5222.
Web site: www.womeninfilmvideo.org (seminars, screenings)

Writers Guild of America, east: 555 West 57th Street, New York, NY 10019. Phone: (212) 767-7800.
Web site: www.wga.org (writers' union, script registration, resources, seminars, and more)

Writers Guild of America, west: 7000 West 3rd Street, Los Angeles, CA 90048. Phone: (323) 951-4000 or (800) 548-4532.
Web site: www.wga.org (writers' union, script registration, resources, seminars, and more)

MARKETING GUIDES

Hollywood Access Directory:
Web site: www.hollydex.com (online listings for agents, managers, production companies, and more)

The Hollywood Agents and Managers Directory: 3000 West Olympic Boulevard, Suite 2525, Santa Monica, CA 90404. Phone (310) 315-4815 or (800) 815-0503.
Web site: www.hollyvision.com (lists agents and managers on the East and West coasts)

The Hollywood Creative Directory: 3000 West Olympic Boulevard, Suite 2525, Santa Monica, CA 90404. Phone (310) 315-4815 or (800) 815-0503.
Web site: www.hollyvision.com (lists studios, networks, production companies and executives with phone, fax, addresses, selected produced credits, staff and titles.)

The Hollywood Reporter Blu-Book Film, TV, and Commercial Production Directory: The Hollywood Reporter, 5055 Wilshire Boulevard, Suite 600, Los Angeles, CA 90036. Phone: (323) 525-2150.
Web site: www.hollywoodreporter.com (lists production companies, executives, talent, and more)

Writers Guild of America: Guild Signatory Agent and Agencies Online: Film, TV, and interactive agents.
Web site: www.wga.org (agent directory)

WHERE TO BUY PUBLISHED SCREENPLAYS

Look under "Screenplays" on the Internet and you will find links to assist you in your search. Also, major bookstores carry published scripts.

Hollywood Book City: 6627 Hollywood Boulevard, Hollywood, CA 90028. Phone: (323) 466-2525.
Web site: www.hollywoodbookcity.com (also lists additional store locations)

Hollywood Legends: 49 Greenwich Avenue, New York, NY 10014. Phone: (212) 243-9935.
(they do not have a Web site, but they will mail/e-mail their script directory)

Lone Eagle Publishing Company: 1024 North Orange Drive, Hollywood, CA 90038. Phone: (323) 308-3400 or (800) FILMBKS.
Web site: www.loneeagle.com

Script City: 8033 Sunset Boulevard, Suite 1500, Hollywood, CA 90046. Phone: (800) 676-2522.
Web site: www.scriptcity.net

ScriptShop.com: P.O. Box 11742, Atlanta, GA 30355. Phone: (770) 234-4000.
Web site: www.scriptshop.com

ADDITIONAL RESOURCES

Contact your state arts council and local film commissions for grants and other opportunities.

The Writers Guild of America (WGA) provides extensive resources for researching information about your script: 1) FYI Listings: organizations (such as Air Force, medical, educational, psychological, and religious) that provide free research information to WGA members; 2) WGA Research Links for non-members; 3) Membership Directory.

The Directors Guild of America (DGA) and the **Writers Guild of America (WGA)** publish membership listings.

ABOUT THE AUTHOR

Susan Kouguell is chairperson of Su-City Pictures East, a motion picture consulting company founded in 1990. Her international clients include independent writers, filmmakers, and production companies, as well as the major studios, including Miramax, Warner Bros., and Fine Line Features. She co-wrote with Carl Capotorto *The Suicide Club* (Anjelica Films), wrote voice-over narrations for *Murder One* and *Dakota* (Miramax), and has done eleven feature film rewrites. A two-time finalist for the Sundance Screenwriters Laboratory, she has received fifteen screenwriting and film production grants and fellowships from the Jerome Foundation, the MacDowell Colony, the New York Foundation for the Arts, the Edward Albee Foundation, and others. Six of her short internationally award-winning films (made in collaboration with Ernest Marrero) are in the archives and permanent collection of the Museum of Modern Art and were included in the Whitney Museum of American Art Biennial. Kouguell worked with director Louis Malle on the documentary *And the Pursuit of Happiness*, and was the screenplay doctor and associate producer of the features *Rum & Coke*, directed by Maria Escobedo, and Jay Craven's *Where the Rivers Flow North*.

Kouguell teaches screenwriting at the Harvard University Extension School and Tufts University, and taught screenwriting at the School of Visual Arts. She has presented numerous film industry seminars to organizations and universities, including the Writers Guild of America, Directors Guild of America, Independent Feature Project, New York Women in Film & Television, Atlantic Film & Video Producers Conference in Canada, New England Screenwriters Conference, NYU, Temple University, The New School, The Reel School, Emerson, Hunter, and Purchase Colleges.

ORDER FORM

Please send the following:

	PRICE	QTY.	TOTAL
☐ The Savvy Screenwriter	$14.95	_____	_____
☐ The Hit List	$39.95	_____	_____

Subtotal $ _____

*Shipping & Handling $ _____

TOTAL $ _____

*US Shipping: $4.95 for first book or disk, $2.95 for each additional product.
International: $9.95 for first book or disk, $5.95 for each additional product.

Please send free information on:

☐ Su-City Pictures Consulting

☐ Speaking/Seminars

☐ The Hit List Software

Payment Information

☐ Check/Money Order (Payable to TL Hoell Books)

Charge My   ☐ Visa   ☐ MasterCard   ☐ AMEX

Card Holder's Name _____

Card Number _____ Exp. Date _____

Signature _____

Daytime Phone _____ E-mail address _____

Shipping Information

Name _____

Address _____

City _____ State _____ Zip _____ Country _____

Ordering Information

Fax Orders: (603) 773-9677   E-mail Orders: info@tlhoellbooks.com
World Wide Web Orders: www.savvyscreenwriter.com
Mail Orders: TL Hoell Books, 1 Colonial Way, Exeter, NH 03833